Creepy Corners
Searching for Truth in Paranormal Claims

By Carolyn Dougherty

Cover art by Jim Roldan.

PUBLISHED BY COSMIC PANTHEON PRESS

www.cosmicpantheon.com

PROUDLY PRINTED IN THE USA!

ISBN: 978-0-9834369-5-9

CAROLYN DOUGHERTY

CONTENTS

CREEPY CORNERS

PREFACE

Welcome to my personal journey into the world of paranormal investigating. Over the 20 or so years since I had my first paranormal experience, I went from believing every claim at face value to actively discovering there are a number of common natural explanations for so-called hauntings. Along the way, many of my personal beliefs have been challenged, and even transformed. I still do not have all the answers. There are cases where I can't find a sound explanation for what I personally experienced. So that is why I am still searching.....

There is a lot of conflicting information out there about paranormal investigating. There is no official "ghost hunting school" so I am lucky that various investigators across the country were willing to mentor me in my quest to learn about, and eventually become, a paranormal investigator. I hope this book can serve as a good starting point for those who are interested in learning about paranormal investigating.

A couple of years ago I started an educational blog called Carolyn's Creepy Corner to help combat the mountain of misinformation that plagues the paranormal field. My blog has a small following on Facebook, where some fellow paranormal enthusiasts suggested I rework it into book form in order to reach a wider audience. So here you go. I hope it will inspire you to search for your own answers.

CAROLYN DOUGHERTY

ACKNOWLEDGEMENTS

Many heartfelt thanks to the following people who have supported me and my so-called "weird hobby":

My husband Dan (I love you and promise to haunt you if I croak first), my parents Ed and Shirley, my siblings Tom and Frances, my BFF Joy, my friends at MyPara (especially Rick, Jon, Red and Matt), The Ghost Society LLC, all the fellow investigators who have shared information and advice with me, readers of my blog, everyone who has shared their paranormal experiences with me, my writer friends who offered valuable feedback (especially Debbie, Jim and the Lake Effect Scribes), and finally, George.

CREEPY CORNERS

CHAPTER 1: MY INTRODUCTION TO THE UNKNOWN

The priest, his face grim, left just as night descended on the bleak day. The woman closed the front door behind him and stood there a moment, feeling the weight of her grief. Hushed voices, in French and broken English, drifted from the kitchen as relatives shared memories. Instead of joining them, she turned and made her way down the dark and narrow hall where candlelight leaked from the doorway at the end. She wanted to be alone with him to say goodbye. She paused at the door and took a deep breath. Slowly, she pushed the door open and peered inside the dim room. Her father's body was laid out on the bed, dressed in his Sunday clothes. Shadows jumped from the flickering candles, making him look like he was only sleeping. Tears trickled down her face as she looked at the man who bounced her on his knee when she was a little girl, who walked her down the aisle at her wedding and who later bounced her own children on his knee. She went to the bedside and reached out to touch his hand, but suddenly froze, her eyes wide. Floating above her father was a glowing white mist. It looked like ground fog, but cast off its own light. She gasped and clutched her hands to her chest. "Pére?" she whispered in awe. Then the mist drifted up to the ceiling and dissipated. The woman shook from her roiling emotions. "Pére?" she whispered again.

"It's not the dead you have to worry about. It's the living that can hurt you," my Grandma assured me as she rocked back and forth in her favorite chair.   I was seven or eight years old and was complaining that my older siblings scared me with ghost stories. Up until that day, I thought of ghosts as monsters, like vampires and Frankenstein. It never occurred to me that they had once been regular living people. All that changed when my grandmother told me her own experience after her father's death.

I believe this was the origin of my lifelong fascination with ghosts. Soon after, I ordered books from Scholastic and Reader's Digest where I got my first exposure to well-known ghost lore. I eagerly read about The Winchester Mystery House, of the screaming skull of Burton Agnes Hall, of the ghost ship The Flying Dutchman, of a small house in Bélmez where ghostly faces appeared in the tiles on the floor. I ordered more books to read about Raynham Hall, where the spectral Brown Lady was photographed descending a grand staircase, of poltergeist cases, and of Chicago's infamous hitchhiking haunt, Resurrection Mary. As I grew older, shows featuring paranormal stories began to surface, like Unsolved Mysteries and Sightings. That's where I saw various parapsychologists profiled: Dr. Hans Holzer, Dr. Barry Taff, Dr. William Roll and Loyd Auerbach. I fantasized doing what they did for a living when I grew up. These shows also introduced me to more well-known paranormal cases: The Queen Mary, The Heartland Ghost in Kansas, the case of Heidi in Georgia who talked to ghosts, as well as The Myrtles Plantation in Louisiana and The Moss Beach Distillery in California – both locations that I would visit many years later.

In high school and college, whenever the topic of ghost stories came up, friends would usually shrug them off. However, when talking one on one, I often heard, "I don't believe in that stuff, but I had this weird experience ...." A friend's sister told me she changed dorms because she was living in a former convalescent hospital and heard the sound of a wheelchair rolling up and down her hallway late at night when no one was there. I talked to another friend who would turn white at the mention of ghosts. He claimed he played with a Ouija board with a friend and soon after he was plagued by terrifying experiences in his home until his parents called in a priest. Another friend reported seeing a woman in an old-fashioned nightgown walking down his road where she vanished before his eyes. An elderly neighbor later explained to him that over many years, several people had also seen the woman disappear at the same spot. I believed, and I wanted to experience it for myself.

While still in college, I was a volunteer docent (tour guide) for a historical home that had been turned into a museum. It wasn't hard for my imagination to take hold in that place. It was a time capsule. Most of the original furniture, décor and personal items were kept just as they had been many decades before. As a docent, I had access to rooms closed to the public and one day found an ancient family photo album. Inside were pictures of babies and small children, posed right after their death for macabre mementos. Another picture was of a young woman in a coffin at her wake held in the home's front parlor. These pictures may be chilling to modern sensibilities, but historically, they were common practice. Naturally, this fueled my fancy that ghosts might be hanging around.

There was one room on the second floor that felt "weird." Unlike any other room in the beautiful Victorian home, I felt uneasy every time I went in there. I chalked it up to my overactive imagination and a sinister-looking dress mannequin lurking in the corner. However, I soon observed I wasn't the only one who avoided that room. Whenever it was time to open for visitors or close up for the night, whichever docent I was with would ask me to take care of "that" room. Finally, I asked one lady about it and without meeting my eyes, said, "There's just something about that room that I don't like."

I noticed other odd things, that honestly, could be easily dismissed. When I first worked there, a caretaker lived in the back rooms. A mutual acquaintance told me that he claimed to hear voices and footsteps when alone in that house. Actually, he struck me as a person who might hear voices wherever he was, so I didn't take it too seriously. However, we docents were constantly complaining that objects were not in their places. Since part of our job was cleaning and dusting the artifacts, we knew when they had been moved. I figured the caretaker was the culprit. However, when he moved out and a security system was installed, it continued. Especially in "that" room on the second floor.

One rainy day, since there were no visitors and we weren't conducting tours, another docent and I sat in the kitchen to chat over a cup of coffee. The security system panel was located in there, by the back door. Throughout the house, motion detectors were set up with corresponding lights on the panel. Suddenly the older woman stopped talking midsentence and grabbed my arm. Her eyes were locked on the panel. One by one lights came on: first, the one corresponding to the sensor by the front door, next the one on the staircase, next the one in the second floor hallway and finally, the one across from "that" room. None of the other lights came on. There are only two entrances into the house: the back door where we were sitting and the front door, which was rigged with a bell to alert us to any visitors. That bell never rang that day. We quickly checked the front door and found it closed. We searched the first floor, and found no one. Both of us were nervous, but we went up the stairs together to check the second floor. There was nobody else. We even unlocked and checked the third floor. Again, no one there. We agreed since it was a rainy day anyway, we'd close early and get out of there.

It wasn't the full-body apparition I was hoping for, but I believed I finally had an encounter with something paranormal. It has been 20 years since I worked there, and during that time, so many docents reported odd experiences that the Historical Society agreed to have paranormal teams come in to investigate. Investigators claimed to catch EVPs (Electric Voice Phenomena where voices that aren't heard at the time are recorded and are audible on playback) and strange anomalies in photos. I would love to go back there someday and conduct an investigation to draw my own conclusions.

As the years went by, I continued to read "true" ghost stories. I even started writing down personal accounts from friends and acquaintances. It seemed to me, after talking to these level-headed people, that there had to be something more than overactive imaginations at work here. One friend lived in a house that once belonged to her former teacher. One night she saw her teacher (who had been dead for some time) walking down the hall into the kitchen. She followed her and watched as she opened the china hutch and then vanished. The following morning, my friend woke before the rest of her family and when she went into the kitchen, found the china hutch door open. For her, this ruled out that she had been dreaming. Another woman told me soon after she moved into an old farmhouse, she would often see the ghost of an older woman walk into her kitchen pantry and vanish. She later learned the pantry was originally the door leading to the upstairs before the house had been remodeled and the stairway moved. Another account comes from a woman whose son had come to her scared half to death. He'd been sitting in the living room when he saw a man in overalls and wearing wire rim glasses walk by him and then *through the wall* leading outside. Later, another child was visiting the house. She asked my friend, "Who's that man standing by the barn?" My friend didn't see anyone. The little girl insisted there was a man, wearing overalls "like a farmer" and "old, round" glasses. Once might be imagination, twice coincidence, but three different reports? After the family moved out, a new family with a small boy moved in. The mother saw my friend one day and asked her if she ever had "odd" experiences in that house. My friend asked why. The woman replied that her little boy was scared to go upstairs because he saw "a farmer man" up there.

These stories fueled my interest and I wanted to investigate for myself. So before the current paranormal craze brought about by popular TV shows, I went out and bought a digital camera, cheap EMF (electromagnetic field) detector and a cheap digital recorder. I'm not saying I knew what the heck I was doing with them, but at least I was actively getting out there to see what was going on for me. Luckily, I am married to a very patient and supportive man. While he doesn't share my interest in the paranormal, he is a history buff, so we travel to historical locations where one can often find "ghost tours" or "hunts". This is where I first mistakenly thought I was a real ghost hunter because Icaught "orbs" in my pictures and the guides oohed and aahed over them. I also caught "EVPs" that if you listened really hard, and with some major guesswork, you could make out a phrase after playing it a dozen times or so. My little EMF detector would often go off away from outlets or wiring, so that had to mean there was a ghost there, right?

One trip was to New Orleans. We stayed at an old hotel in the French Quarter. After returning from a scrumptious dinner, we got to our room but my husband's key wouldn't work. Now, this was a real key, not the plastic card keys. I got out my key, and tried it. The lock gave, but the door-knob wouldn't budge. My husband left to retrieve a concierge who arrived with a master key. The same thing happened with him. Finally, he yelled, "Okay guys, this isn't funny any more." The door opened. The concierge looked at our astonished faces and just shrugged. Later that night we took a ghost tour where we learned that long ago, our hotel used to be an orphanage, where, tragically, a fire took the life of many children. Many guests over the years have reported pranks supposedly played by the ghostly children. So who knows? Was it just an old, sticky door-knob? Or something else?

Then, in 2005, a TV show debuted that made me realize I had a lot to learn. The first two seasons of *Ghost Hunters* focused a lot on debunking claims – finding natural causes for experiences. They also focused on using objective techniques in favor of subjective methods that were often profiled in previous paranormal shows. I soon found that all my ghost orb pictures were really pictures of dust, moisture, bugs and other airborne particles. I also learned that EMF meters don't detect ghosts. Like their name implies, they simply detect EMFs and fluctuations within those fields. That doesn't mean there is a ghost around. I also realized there is another dynamic to consider when calling you a paranormal investigator: responsibility to the clients who ask for help. If you don't know what you're doing, you are likely going to mislead them and cause much more harm than any good.

From then on, my focus shifted from learning about ghosts and ghost lore to learning more about the equipment and methodologies used in paranormal investigations. Some may claim there is no "right way" to investigate because at this point, the field is based on theory and speculation. While I agree to some extent, I will say it is wrong to present false evidence to clients because one hasn't taken the time to learn how their equipment works, or about common causes of things often mistaken for paranormal activity, or learning basic protocols to prevent creating images or sounds that can be misinterpreted as anomalies upon review. For example, telling a client a ghostly image was caught when, in reality, it was a very basic camera effect such as lens flare.

A few years later, while my interest turned more toward investigations, I had an experience that reinforced my belief that weird stuff *does* happen now and then.   I was working part time at a retail store. It had recently opened and I was helping the manager put up shelves in the home décor section. While I was on the ladder, I saw a shoe fly off one of the shelves in the shoe department. I don't mean it fell, I mean it launched itself off the shelf! From my vantage point on the ladder, I could see there was no one in that department.   I must have had an odd expression on my face because the manager asked what was wrong.   When I told her what I just saw, instead of her laughing and calling me a nutter, she shrugged and said, "Yeah, that's been happening." She explained that when she or assistant managers unlocked the store in the mornings, they had found shoes on the floor. I immediately went to the shelf and the adjacent storage room looking for signs of a critter or even a mechanical device in case someone was playing a joke. I didn't find anything. There are train tracks and a main road nearby, but I couldn't figure out why the vibration would cause only one shoe to take flight.   Soon it became an inside joke with the workers.

One assistant manager didn't find it so funny. One morning, while she was alone in the store before business hours, a perfume bottle flew towards her. It landed in the middle of the aisle floor, which was tile, and shattered.   The aisle was considerable distance from its shelf, which was on carpet.   If it had somehow fallen off, the bottle would have landed on carpet.   Could it have bounced? Sure, but as far to the middle of the aisle? And with enough force to shatter the bottle? Understandably, she was a bit unnerved. Not long after this, the manager called me to come in on my day off – not to work, but she had something to show me. When I arrived, she took me to the back office where the monitors for the security cameras were. She had opened the store to yet another shoe in the middle of the floor. So she decided to rewind the video. At around 4:30 AM, with the security system confirming no one was in the building, the camera caught the shoe flying off the shelf. Was a ghost with a shoe fetish messing around with the inventory? I don't know. But enough workers had similar experiences there to make me wonder.

Soon afterwards, I went to a TAPS (The Atlantic Paranormal Society profiled on *Ghost Hunters*) event where, over the course of a weekend, they presented various seminars including an overview of basic investigating protocols and equipment and common false positives. Some in the field may scoff because of the association with a TV show, but it was a much better starting point than what too many people in this field do: watch the shows, buy the same gear (without researching it), and copy unreliable or even counterproductive techniques. It prompted me to learn even more before I felt comfortable calling myself an investigator. I did some searching online. On YouTube, I found a couple of informative series. One is Haunted Hoax by Patrick Doyle. Another is by Mike St. Claire. While surfing the net, I also found a

15

networking site called MyPara.net. There I made contact with experienced, informed investigators. Some of them were more than willing to mentor me and answer my questions, particularly with technology. Since I couldn't find what I considered a reliable group in my area, they invited me to visit and investigate with them. Luckily, a couple years ago I saw a blurb in the local newspaper about a relatively new group (it was actually reformed under a new name after some membership changes) and I looked them up online. I saw that they were a science-based team and contacted the founder. He had me fill out an application and scheduled an interview with him and other board members. I was excited when I was accepted into The Ghost Society LLC.

Once I started investigating with them, I learned so much more in a short period of time. There is no better teacher than experience. We investigated historic public buildings, various private businesses, private homes, big buildings, little buildings, old buildings, new buildings. I got hands-on training with my various pieces of equipment, finding out which are more useful and which ones to turn into paperweights. It is one thing to play around on public ghost hunts, it is a whole other situation when you have frightened clients sitting right there, looking to you for answers.

So let me define what paranormal investigating has come to mean for me: looking for valid explanations for paranormal claims. It means keeping an open mind, but accepting that most experiences do have natural causes. One cannot label something paranormal unless one is able to recognize and rule out all other possible causes first. Therefore, attributing every odd sound or shadow to ghosts, or every garbled recording and blurred picture as evidence in order to reinforce one's personal belief in the paranormal is not, in my opinion, true paranormal investigating. It's just wish-fulfillment. That statement might insult some readers, and maybe if I had read that several years ago, I might have been insulted too. But it is an honest assessment, one shared by serious investigators who invest a lot of time, money and effort into research. They utilize science to analyze claims, equipment, data, and methodology. They do this, not because they are "closed-minded" or afraid to think outside the proverbial box, but so that in the event something truly anomalous is discovered, it can be properly studied, and maybe they might find the proof so many of us are looking for.

I am still learning. And searching. Are ghosts real or is science able to explain them away? I don't know, but I'd sure like to find out.

CHAPTER 2: BUMPS IN THE NIGHT

Before we run out to determine whether ghosts are real or not, we first should try to figure out what they are, so that we have better idea of what, exactly, we're looking for.

WHAT, WHY, HOW?

What are ghosts? No one knows for sure, but there are several theories. The most common is that ghosts are the spirits or consciousness of the dead. Some theorize ghosts are psychic imprints on our environment that strong emotions somehow leave a lasting impression that can be sensed long after the fact. Others believe we may experience ghosts due to quantum physics, time slips, or interaction with different dimensions. Still others theorize that ghosts have nothing to do with the dead, but rather the living, and are a product of psychic phenomena. And of course there are those who think ghosts are simply products of misinterpretation, fantasy or fraud.

The debate is nothing new. For example, The Reformation fueled arguments about the nature of ghosts and the afterlife, while during this time secular scholars asserted that ghosts were caused by hoaxes or hysteria. Catholics believed that departed souls went to Purgatory, awaiting Judgment. Prayers were needed to help these souls find Salvation. Some Catholic scholars believed that some ghosts could return and even interact with the living. Protestants, on the other hand, believed there were no Purgatory and that upon death; souls go directly to Heaven or Hell. Because of this, they theorized that ghosts were not human, so they must be demonic. Both sides cited Greek texts for their arguments. Interestingly, early Ancient Greeks believed that the departed were ambivalent towards the living (and vice versa) and that they lingered near their tombs. (Ever wonder where the persistent notion that cemeteries are haunted came from?) Gradually, as commerce opened new trade routes with various cultures and their lore was integrated, Greek ghost stories changed where ghosts became actively connected with the living, eventually becoming agents who could intercede on the living's behalf.

Ghost stories are alluring because they are often highly dramatic, touching on our strongest emotions. They commonly incorporate themes of love and hate, grief and regret, revenge and jealousy, and fear and even salvation.

One thing is certain about ghosts: they are archetypes found in cultures around the world. There are also universal themes to ghost stories, which explain why ghosts are so entrenched in our collective psyche.

ANCESTRAL GHOSTS

Ancestral ghosts are the spirits/souls of the dearly departed family and community members. In many cultures, they are considered a part of the living family and serve as a link to traditions and history. For Native Americans, in many tribal traditions, the dead are called upon for help with crops, fighting illness and bringing rain. For example, every July the Hopi hold the festival *Niman Kachina*. *Kachinas* are ancestral spirits. The Hopi wear masks to symbolize the *Kachinas* and ask for intercession to the gods. In Mexico, the *Dia de Muertos* Day of the Dead, mixes Native cultural traditions (including an Aztec festival celebrating the Queen of the Undeworld and the Catholic faith). Alters are set up in homes where food and gifts are offered to dead loved ones and families visit the graves. While the original aboriginal festival was held in August, it was moved to correspond with the Catholic Feast of All Soul's Day on Nov. 2nd when the deceased faithful are remembered and honored.

In most African religions, they believe in ancestral spirits and that they actively intervene to protect their communities. Like Native Americans, ancestral ghosts are believed to intercede for their families and communities for protection from disease and harm. They help provide rain, crops and abundant game. They are called on to heal illness. Honoring the departed is a part of daily life in many traditions. For example, symbolic food and drink are offered to the sprits. However, if a family or tribe member offends the ancestors, misfortune will follow. Voodoo is a hybrid of African and Catholic traditions, where ancestral ghosts are an integral part.

Asian traditions also include ancestral ghosts. In China, ancestral spirits are considered to be active family members. During feasts, a place is set at the table for the deceased. In Japan, *Reikon* are ancestral spirits. Every July is the *Obon* Festival when the dead return to visit relatives. Lanterns are lit at home to guide spirits in. The *Bon-odori* dances are performed to welcome the spirits.   At the end of the festival, lanterns are lit and placed on the water to guide them back to the other side.

In both Ancient and Modern Rome: *Manes* are sprits of the dead who watch over the living. They continue to advise and protect their living family and community members.

OMEN GHOSTS

Fear of death is primal. Before advances in medicine, the cause of diseases, especially those with a sudden onset, were a mystery. By our nature, we desire an explanation.   Omen ghosts help to fill this need.

In Irish lore the *Banshee* is a harbinger of death, believed to be a ghost related to the family it visits. If she is heard, someone in the house will die.

Those who see her are the ones to die.   While Banshees are most often associated with shrieking, if the doomed are good natured, she sings a sad, but pleasant song. But if not, then she shrieks. Scotland and Wales have their own versions as did the ancient Assyrians. An *Ekimmu* was the ghost of a victim of a violent death who would wail outside of a house, signifying someone in that home is about to die.

Doppelganger is a German term for an apparition that appears as one's double and indicates the person's imminent death. It is called a *Fetch* in England and Ireland. A *wraith* is a Scottish omen of death. Sometimes it is depicted as a person's double, like the *Doppelganger*, but in other versions it is described as a tall, cloaked figure either having no face or the face of a skull.   And in still other variations of the lore, they are only seen in reflections.

In Finnish lore, a *Liekko* is a spectral light that lures travelers to unsafe areas. It is believed to be a spirit of a dead child buried in the forest and it is an omen of death or disaster to those who encounter it.

VENGEFUL GHOSTS

Some ghost stories reflect the morality of a culture and their view of death.   Stories of vengeful ghosts often deal with violent and unjust deaths.

In Japan the *Yurei* are vengeful ghosts who linger after their death. They are often victims of murder or suicide, and they are tied to the physical plane and transformed by their anger or jealousy. *The Grudge* is a movie depicting this type of ghost.

In Arabic lore: an *afrit* is the ghost of a murdered person intent on avenging their death. Similarly, a *Bhut*, or *Bhuta* in Hindu lore is an evil ghost, whose death is usually associated with suicide, execution or accident.

An *angiak* is found in Inuit lore. It is the ghost of a child deliberately left to die in the snow. It will appear to parents and other tribe members unless they move away from the site shortly after its death. The baby's wailing will haunt the entire tribe.

HOUSE SPIRITS

House spirits are attached to one's home. In many traditions, they can wreak havoc on the household if displeased. This helps explain when there is an odd noise or flicker of the lights, why some people jump to the conclusion that a ghost is responsible.

In East India nats are found throughout every home. They hide in corners and in closets. The *Bommasso* can be spirits of the dead, who are feared, so proper burial rites, must be followed.

A *domovik* is a Russian household spirit, found in every home. Generally, it lives behind the stove, where it watches over the family. But if the family upsets or disrespects it, it will become destructive, breaking objects and perhaps even burning the house down. When it is seen, it appears as an old man. In some versions he is the original patriarch of that family.

Kobolds or *Kobalts* are house spirits found in Germany, Austria, Denmark, Sweden and Switzerland. If they are in a good mood, they will help inhabitants, but are often mischievous and if provoked or disrespected, like the *domovik*, will become destructive and turn on the family. They can also be found in mines. They will help lead the miners to a productive area. If they are not rewarded with gifts, they will become vengeful and cause cave-ins. These ghosts are akin to Great Britain's *goblins*.

Lares were protective spirits of ancient Rome, found in every home. Today, some Italians still see them on occasion. They are friendly to the occupants of the house, but antagonistic to strangers.

In Scotland, Urisks are house spirits who help with tasks, but are never seen except by those with "second sight". Every Manor house would keep an unoccupied seat in the kitchen for the *Urisk*. In England, they are called *brownies*.

For a more complete list of ghosts across the globe, read *The Weiser Field Guide to Ghosts, Apparitions, Spirits,*

CREEPY CORNERS

Spectural Lights and Other Hauntings of History and Legend by Raymond Buckland.

So.... we have theories of what ghosts may be and why they might haunt the living. But just HOW are we supposed to prove they exist that would satisfy science and skeptics? The cryptozoologists searching for Bigfoot have a couple of advantages: they know they are looking for a flesh-and-blood biological creature, presumably an unknown bipedal primate. Secondly, they have tangible evidence to work with, such as footprints and hair samples that can be analyzed by qualified scientists. Ghost hunters don't have such luxuries. We don't know what ghosts are or what they are made of, which presents the main challenge of paranormal investigating. Because of this, **we have to first prove what they *aren't.***

GHOSTS AND MISPERCEPTION

After a long day, you're sitting alone at home one night, comfortably reading a book in a cozy chair in front of a crackling fireplace. Thunder rumbles in the distance and the room is briefly illuminated as lightening spills though the window blinds. You continue reading when another flash fills the room but this time, out of the corner of your eye, you see the outline of a figure standing by the window. Gasping, you turn to look.... and it's gone! Shocked, you get up and turn on more lights, which only reveal nothing. Then you feel the prickle of goose bumps on your skin as you realize you've just seen a ghost.

.... But did you? Is it possible your eyes played tricks on you? With certain environmental and physiological factors, the answer is yes. Misperception can be a touchy subject, but those who are interested in investigating paranormal claims should have a basic understanding of common causes contributing to such experiences. We cannot honestly identify something as paranormal if we are not able to recognize, and therefore rule out, natural causes first.

It is understandable that people might become defensive when presented with the possibility that they did not actually experience what they thought they did. It is extremely uncomfortable to know that we cannot trust our own senses. After all, we rely on our senses to inform us about our environment as well as our status in it. Some may be concerned that misperception might be sign of a mental or emotional defect. This is untrue. If someone experienced a hallucination because they were severely dehydrated, is that a mental defect? Of course not, it is a physiological issue.

Sometimes, under certain conditions, our own physiology fails us. When visual and audio information is inadequate for the brain to interpret, it relies on our memory and experience to fill in the missing data. Unfortunately, sometimes that process results in misinterpretation.

Everyone experiences unintentional blindness. When we become focused on a task, or go into "autopilot" we can miss significant details right in front of us. In some studies of this phenomenon, subjects failed to see a person walk into the room. This is actually a defense mechanism for the brain because if we consciously tried to process all the sensory input available in our environment, we'd go insane. Many times, I have heard claims where people said they were busy doing something and when they returned to a room (like a kitchen) a cupboard door was now open, and they swore it wasn't before. Maybe a ghost opened it, but another explanation is that it might have been left open by a living person and was not noticed before when the person's attention was focused elsewhere.

Many of us are familiar with the term matrixing, also known as pareidolia. Our brain is programmed to recognize patterns. When processing information, it will try to make a pattern out of random data. Michael Shermer, psychologist and founder of Skeptic Magazine, refers to this as Patternicity. In his book, *The Believing Brain*, he asserts it can be traced back through our evolution, serving as a basic survival mechanism when our ancestors walked the savannas of Africa. A visual example of matrixing is when we find shapes in the clouds. Our brain is especially fond of finding faces, which causes some issues with so-called ghost photos. People will see "faces" in curtains, window reflections, etc. and mistake it for being paranormal. Pareidolia also occurs in how we process audio. One very common example is when one is taking a shower and thinks they hear the phone ringing, but it isn't. We hear a sound at a certain frequency, and again, our brain runs through our memory files to identify it. Sometimes it picks something else that is at a similar frequency, in this case a phone ringing, instead of the reverberation of the running shower.

The brain interprets sound in three general modes: random noise (ambient sound), music and speech. The only information received from our ears is amplitude frequency and the time the sound arrives. The brain then takes over, and interprets what the sounds are, using context and expectation based on recognized patterns. So the brain differentiates the three modes based on pattern recognition. Therefore, if ambient noise contains frequencies and rhythms similar to speech, the brain will switch modes and try to interpret the sound as speech.

Have you heard the term "babbling brook?" Running water can often sound like someone talking. During one investigation, a client claimed to hear whispering when she was in her bedroom. A couple of us did hear what sounded like whispering in there. However, when we were in the hallway, we could hear a fish tank filter from an adjacent room. To be sure that was the cause, we turned it off (just for a couple minutes; the fish were fine). The "whispering" stopped.

CREEPY CORNERS

There are other factors to consider when trying interpreting speech. Have you noticed when recordings of supposed EVPs are played, people often have different interpretations of what is being said? As discussed in *Spook* by Mary Roach, psychologists can explain this with the verbal transformation effect. B.F. Skinner received his Ph.D. from Harvard, where he remained as a researcher and professor of Psychology. In addition to psychology, he did research in linguistics. In one experiment, he played random sequences of vowels and asked to report if they heard something meaningful. Subjects not only reported words with consonants (remember only vowels were used) they were convinced they interpreted the words correctly. C. Maxwell Cade, a physicist for the British government, also conducted an experiment where subjects were asked to transcribe what they were told was a poor-quality recording of a lecture. Subjects deciphered phrases and entire sentences. But the recording was in fact nothing but white noise.

The physiology of our eyes and how they function often plays a part in misperception. It is our central vision (produced by retinal cone cells) that provides details of what we see. Our peripheral vision (produced by retinal rod cells) excels at perceiving movement, but lacks details and color. Our brain then helps "fill in" the missing details so we don't notice. Sometimes the brain substitutes images from our memory banks. Unfortunately, the substituted image may not be accurate and what is a simple shadow may become an apparition. When we turn to look at it head on, it vanishes because our central vision now processes the details, and the substituted image our brain created is no longer needed.

Another misperception is a product of a common optical illusion. Certain patterns, such as alternating black and white stripes, cause a motion illusion known as the peripheral drift illusion where peripheral vision sees movements in such patterns. So banisters, blinds and shutters all have the potential to cause this effect.

Low light conditions amplify these phenomena. Our eyes aren't designed well for night vision. It takes our eyes at least half an hour to adjust to see as well as we can in the dark. Since our retinal cone cells don't function well in the dark, our central vision will be poor and we have to rely on our peripheral vision. And because our peripheral vision is lacking when it comes to processing details and color well, this poses significant potential for misperception. In dark or low light conditions we don't interpret the shape of objects as accurately, and we don't see color well enough which may cause objects to look like shadows or even white lights, and we have poor depth perception. Another optical illusion, which can occur in dark conditions, is autokinesis: if you stare at small objects for too long, they appear to move. This can also occur if you stare at lights, such as those produced by LED displays. As mentioned before, our peripheral vision's strength is detecting movement. However, without the detailed central vision functioning well, our ability to see exactly where the moving object is will be poor. It is not difficult to understand how easy it is for misperception to occur. Add suggestibility to the mix and you have a recipe for seeing ghosts. Another possible issue to be aware of is that sitting in total darkness for a prolonged period of time is a form of sensory deprivation, which can also cause mild hallucinations.

Hallucinations are often associated with drugs or mental illness, but they also occur because of fairly common conditions. People might think hallucinations are just limited to "seeing things" that aren't there in reality. But hallucinations can be visual, auditory, olfactory, and tactile or a combination. There are physiological conditions that can cause any healthy, sane person to hallucinate. For example, fatigue, sleep deprivation, stress, and dehydration can cause hallucinations.

Certain environmental factors also can be attributed to inducing hallucinations. Prolonged exposure to certain electromagnetic fields may trigger hallucinations and it has been reported that some people who may be more sensitive to high electromagnetic fields also experience feelings of being watched, anxiety, headaches and even tingling of the skin. Other possible triggers include prolonged exposure to significant levels of radon, mold or carbon monoxide. Obviously, such conditions can be found in homes and should be evaluated where there are claims of paranormal activity.

Infrasound is another environmental contributor of hallucinations. Infrasound occurs at a frequency below 20 Hertz. We don't hear it, but we can still perceive it. Infrasound not only is known to cause visual and auditory disturbances and hallucinations but also causes feelings of dread, anxiety, nausea and "heaviness" of the atmosphere. Obviously this can be misperceived as something paranormal. There are many common causes of infrasound, both from man-made and natural sources. Trains, heavy traffic, heavy machinery, and industrial plants all are sources of man-made infrasound. Natural sources include thunderstorms, waves crashing, running rivers, and fault lines. It is important to note that basements act like resonance boxes, amplifying sounds, including infrasound. Same goes for large box-like buildings such as hospitals, schools, warehouses and prisons. If they are abandoned and mostly empty, this obviously increases the reverberation within the structure.

Some of the most common claims of paranormal activity involve people waking in the middle of the night to see a figure standing by their bed and then it vanishes. While this is certainly a startling and disturbing experience, there are scientific explanations which have been observed in sleep laboratory studies. There are hallucinations that are associated with fairly common sleep disturbances, specifically when one part of the brain is in a waking state while another part is in a dreaming state. Hypnagogic hallucinations occur when a person is falling asleep and hypnopompic hallucinations occur as a person is waking up. Common examples of such hallucinations included feeling touched, hearing someone speaking (most commonly one's name being called), feeling a "presence" in the room, seeing gray or light "blobs" levitating in the air, smelling smoke or perfume, and as mentioned before, seeing a person or other kind of entity (i.e., aliens or demon) in the room. Fatigue, sleep deprivation, change in sleep patterns, some medications, and stress, are all factors that increase the odds of having such an experience. This is why I think so many hotels are "haunted". Many people get stressed and fatigued from their travels, and tend not to sleep well in strange surroundings. This presents conditions that can trigger hypnagogic and hypnopompic hallucinations. As someone who used to suffer from this type of sleep disorder as a child, I can assure you that the experience feels very real.

A related but more frightening sleep disorder is sleep paralysis. In addition to the hypnagogic/hypnopompic hallucination, the subject is also unable to move their body. They feel like something is holding them down or sitting on their chest. In some severe cases, the hallucination takes form of a paranormal entity, such as a ghost, witch or demon who is assaulting the subject. The subject may try, but cannot speak or cry out. Then after a few minutes, both the paralysis and "entity" vanish. This disorder certainly fits the profile of the incubus/succubus or "night hag" phenomenon reported over the centuries. It remains one of the most common claims reported to paranormal investigators.

While the paranormal may exist, it is important that paranormal investigators are aware of, and are able to identify, common probable causes of misperception. They might not help the client get rid of a ghost, but they might give them peace of mind by providing alternative explanations for their experiences. And if investigators are able to rule out such explanations, what is left might be truly paranormal.

To learn more about misperceptions, go to ASSAP's website (see *Sources and Recommended Reading* at the end of this book) and read the following articles by Marurice Townsend: *How People See Ghosts*, Near *Sleep Experiences* and *Corner of the Eye Phenomena*

FALSE POSITIVES

Those who are serious about paranormal investigating and research need to become familiar with common causes of false positives in evidence. Unfortunately, there are even "seasoned" investigators who don't (or won't) become familiar with their equipment and proper investigative protocols and still put out "evidence" that have common, explainable (and reproducible) causes.

I am not an expert in technical equipment, but I constantly study articles and books from those who are. There are those in this field who have taken the time to test equipment in and out of the field, analyze how devices work, and complete experiments to reproduce false positives. These are the people we should be learning from, not TV stars. Please refer to *Sources and Recommended Reading* at the end of this book.

SEEING IS NOT BELIEVING

The most common false positive, and a big pet peeve of many investigators, is the orb. Concerning progress in the field of paranormal research, it is counterproductive to still cling to the unfounded notion that orbs are ghosts. There is NO concrete, objective, or credible evidence that orbs are ghosts. However, there is plenty of evidence, (which can be reliably replicated in experiments) that orbs are caused by dust, dead skin, (ew!) insulation, pollen, lint, bugs and moisture. There are reports that people have seen orbs with the naked eye, and so people conclude those must be "real" orbs. They may be "real" but there is no proof that they are ghosts. What they likely are, which has been reliably observed, is ball lightning or another form of plasmoid. Our environment is saturated with electromagnetic fields. Add some static electricity, ions and other components in the atmosphere and you have a recipe for an orb. Some who want to cling to their orbs will argue, "But I caught an EVP when this picture was taken." Okay... but a haunted house, just like a non-haunted house, will have dust in it. There is no direct connection to the EVP. For sake of argument, let's say some of those orbs ARE ghosts. At this point we don't have the technology that can differentiate between pictures of ghost orbs and those caused by common airborne particles, so therefore, we cannot present such pictures as true evidence. It would be highly irresponsible to have a client scared in their own home because of dust bunnies.

Other common false positives are also related to people not understanding how their cameras work or process images. Lens flares can create an "orb" or other anomalous light. All it takes is for a light source to be directed towards your camera. The source may not even be in frame. (A good reason to take control shots). There also are many photos floating around the internet that supposedly contain "vortices". First off, to date, no one has proven energy vortices even exist. I personally believe in the possibility on their existence, just not in Aunt Betty's closet. Most of these "vortices" are easily identified by photographic experts as camera straps, hair, or a thread that got too close to the camera lens. Another common false positive is "ghostly mists". Again, after analysis, many of these mists turn out to be cigarette smoke, ordinary ground fog, smoke from candles, or breath. Breath on a cold night can be deceiving; even if you "hold your breath" while taking the picture, your exhale can show up a good 30 or more seconds after.

CREEPY CORNERS

Sometimes shadows that seem anomalous show up in photos and videos. But again, after analysis, sometimes these are due to the function of the camera trying to "focus" in low light. Add some matrixing, the phenomena where the brain tries to interpret vague information into something recognizable, and you can have a shadow person.

Light streaks are another common anomaly that shows up in photos. Again, many of these are explained by long exposure in low light conditions. Lights from LED displays, flashlights, or outside light sources, can be captured as streaks in such conditions. Flying bugs and falling debris reflecting from the flash can also create streaks.

Some teams use high-priced gadgets to convince others (or themselves) they have the capability to capture spirit energy on film. Once such device is the PIP (Polycontrast Interference Photography) camera. The claim is it can photograph bioenergy and spirit energy. In reality, all evidence points to it photographing light variances which change with the slightest movement of the subject and fluctuation in the lighting.

Besides learning about how your camera functions, here are a couple of techniques I use to reduce false positives in photos: First, take control shots, with good lighting, in the areas you will be investigating. Second, when taking pictures during the investigation, take at least three shots in rapid succession. If you have an anomaly that shows up in one, but not the others, and it does not show up in the control shot, the odds are a bit higher that you caught something interesting.

DO YOU HEAR WHAT I HEAR?

False positives come in audio form as well. We are so used to TV shows where they catch a supposed EVP in every episode. Many teams I know who use higher-end recorders and strict protocols claim they get only a few EVPs they consider valid evidence per YEAR. Why the discrepancy?

Proper protocols are necessary to produce credible EVPs. There are too many ways to easily create false positives. One way is holding the recorder during the session. If you rub your finger against the recorder, or rub the recorder against your clothes, you will catch a sound that can be misinterpreted as speech. Walking around during EVPs can also capture sounds that can sound like speech. Clothes rubbing, shoes scraping on the floor, etc. are common cause of false positives. Cheaper digital recorders also can create digital artifacts, which again, can be misinterpreted. "Tagging" is absolutely essential for good EVP work. Ambient sounds like a stomach growling, a sigh, someone shifting their weight, etc. can all be heard as speech. Avoid whispering during investigations because on review, it can be misidentified. Just talk at a normal volume.

CREEPY CORNERS

Many groups invest time and money in video recording their EVP sessions. This way, if an anomaly is heard, they can cross-reference the video to see if there is a mundane cause of the sound. In order to present credible evidence, you need to first scrutinize it thoroughly. Believe me, once it's out there, someone else will!

Another problem critics have with cheaper digital recorders is the possibility of recording radio frequencies. These not only could come from local radio stations, but CB radios and cell phones as well. The higher end recorders have internal shielding to help prevent this.

So you take all the precautions and still you catch what sounds like someone talking. Is it a legitimate EVP? Not necessarily. Remember, sometimes background noise can be misinterpreted by the brain as speech. The brain basically recognizes sounds in three general categories: music, ambient noise and speech. If the frequencies, patterns, or harmonics produced by background noise is similar enough to speech, our brain may hear it as such and try to "fill in" words where there are none. So make sure you tag background noise such as a furnace running, or running water, etc.

You can find great information about EVPs and recorders at the website *Jim's Destinations* (see *Sources and Recommended Reading*).

Acoustics can be crazy. At the Burlington County Prison in New Jersey, there is small section with three cells. During a public investigation, my husband and I repeated an experiment featured on Ghost Hunters. If a person whispers inside the third cell, you can CLEARLY hear what they are saying if you stand inside the first cell. However, if you stand in the hall or the middle cell, you can't hear them. My husband and I tested this and found it to be an interesting phenomenon. However, we couldn't find a good explanation when we played back the audio from an EVP session in the women's wing and heard a baby's cry. We didn't hear it at the time, and there were no babies or small children present that evening. I later learned that babies were indeed housed with their mothers there.

GHOST DETECTORS

Okay, there is no such thing. However, a lot of people seem to think EMF detectors do just that. They do not. They simply detect electromagnetic fields and fluctuations in those fields. Again, it is important to learn how the device works, what it is detecting, and what can affect it.

There are good EMF detectors out there. I prefer the Mel Meter because it detects both AC and DC and is a tri-axis meter. It also comes equipped with an ambient thermometer and in some models, a geophone feature. Less gadgets to carry around. However, it is important to know what can cause "spikes" and fluctuations to avoid calling something paranormal when it isn't. Compressors and motors may cycle before they come on and off. This is true in furnaces, air conditioners, refrigerators, water heaters, etc. As they cycle (which you most likely won't hear and be aware of) they will throw off higher EMFs. So be aware of this when a spike seems to occur for no reason. If you get a spike and a minute or so later the furnace comes on or off, you can rule it out as paranormal. Also, certain factors in the environment can affect fields, such as decaying metals, running water through pipes, and the vibration of certain metals such as iron and steel. So if there is a metal roof rattling in the wind, it can throw off your readings. Also, if anything is statically charged, it can affect readings. Dust, in the right conditions, can be statically charged, so if you get a reading in correlation with seeing an "orb" in your viewfinder, please be aware of this.

The Trifield Natural reads DC (direct current) and filters out man-made AC (alternating currents). Human beings have DC field. So to use this properly, it needs to be stationary and away from human contamination. It is not reliable for sweeps, even though a popular TV cast has used it in this manner. Because they read natural EMFs, they are affected by environmental and atmospheric conditions. Running water (like underground streams), moving or vibrating iron or steel (like passing traffic or a moving elevator), thunderstorms, solar flares, and geomagnetic storms can affect the device and cause false positives.

MACHINES THAT GO "BING"

There are various gadgets being widely used on paranormal investigations (thanks to them being profiled on TV shows). While some credible investigators (including some friends of mine) have had what they felt were interesting experiences with some of these, there are many factors that can affect the devices and create false positives. At best, these gadgets should be considered "experimental" and any results from them should not be presented as evidence, especially to clients.

THE K-II METER

Yeah, I admit it. I ran out and bought one after I saw what seemed to be an impressive session on TV several years ago. However since then, many investigators have found serious flaws in using these as valid investigative tools. First off, it's not that great of an EMF meter. It only operates as a single axis EMF detector, rather than the preferred three-axis. Second, it is very sensitive to radio frequencies, and picks up local CBs, cell phones, WiFi, Bluetooth, etc. So any "hits" may be a teen within range texting her friends instead of a ghost manipulating the EMF field. Third, and this will come up again, K-II "conversations" are primed for misinterpretation. Apophena is a term used to describe how our brain likes to make patterns out of random data. So during a K-II session, you may have 2 or 3 direct "responses" to your questions, but people conveniently forget the 45 times questions got no response or the K-II lit up randomly. Some people desperately try to rationalize this, saying the spirits only have so much energy to answer certain questions, or they only respond to certain people because of their "frequency", etc. There is absolutely no evidence to support these claims.

To read more about the faults of the K-II Meter, please read *The K-II Meter vs. Science* by Vince Wilson at the Haunted Cottage (see *Sources and Recommended Reading*).

FLASHLIGHT COMMUNICATION

The same goes with flashlight "communication" sessions. In addition to remembering only the "hits" and downplaying the "misses", there are too many factors that can affect the performance of the flashlight. First off, when you loosen the flashlight to make it "easier" for spirits to manipulate it, you also make it easier for any vibrations to set it off. There have been experiments done that suggest it is the heat of the light itself which causes it to go on and off as the internal connections contract and expand. I know for a fact, after conducting several experiments using different Maglites in various conditions, they will come on and off "by themselves" as they cool down and heat up. Now, if a flashlight that has NOT been altered or manipulated in any way goes on and off by it, then I will be impressed.

I know reliable investigators who experiment with flashlight communication. (The operative word being "experiment" – they don't present it as evidence".) However, unlike what's typically portrayed on TV, they use controls, carefully record the hits and misses, and use statistical inference to analyze the results. While I remain skeptical, there was one session that made me say, "Hmmm?" I was in a blacksmith's shop in a historical village. The story was that the blacksmith, facing poverty, committed suicide in the shop. There were multiple flashlights used and it was cold: around 30 degrees inside, 4 degrees outside. A few flashlights flickered randomly during the questions. I wasn't at all impressed. After a while, none of them turned on. So I asked, "Do you want us to leave?" A flashlight in the center of the table, which had not turned on at all during the previous 40 minutes, immediately came on at full beam. It stayed on until I said, "Okay, we'll go now" and then it immediately shut off. Could be coincidence. Maybe someone manipulated it somehow. Or maybe, that poor blacksmith just wanted to be left alone.

FRANK'S BOX AND SHACK HACKS

Frank Sumption is a UFO enthusiast who created a device that reportedly sweeps radio frequencies to search for signals from extraterrestrials. Eventually, the device caught the attention of paranormal researchers who came up with the theory that spirits can manipulate the radio frequencies, and use them to communicate. Those who couldn't make their own, or afford a Frank's Box, began to violate defenseless AM/FM radios. They bought inexpensive Radio Shack radios and modified them to continually sweep the stations, hence the term Shack Hack. Again, audio matrixing comes into play with these devices. As mentioned before, when our brain is in speech mode, it tries very hard to make words from nonsense. While the dial sweeps back and forth, we hear phonemes, the very basic forms of speech. Sometimes we think we hear a word or even a phrase. There is a common phenomenon that explains this: phonemic restoration effect, the perceptual completion of a familiar pattern. C@n y*u re^d th#s? Similar to reading text with missing or substituted letters, we will hear sounds that have been omitted or substituted from words as if they were actually present. Add cognitive bias and people will hear words or even responses. I have sat in on a few sessions, and I found it interesting that people would interpret "responses" very differently. Another issue, mentioned earlier, is apophena. If people do hear a recognizable word they will strive to make it relevant. I witnessed this during a session one summer. Among a stream of random words, we heard the word "soldier". So some people were convinced we were communicating with a dead soldier. The problem though, is that it was Memorial Day weekend, and the odds that discussions on radio stations would have included the word "soldier" were pretty high.

THE OVILUS

This is a device that has a set of programmed words. The theory is that spirits can manipulate the device and choose words to communicate. Going back to the word of the day, apophena, listeners will strive to make the words relevant. Many of the words I have heard used by the device can be applied in many situations. Take "water" for example. Chances are you are in a location that has water somewhere in the vicinity.

I also have problem with the theory behind this. I doubt a spirit who died before our current technological age can suddenly learn how to manipulate complex electronic components. Maybe there is a how-to handbook on the other side, but I doubt it. Personally, I am a tech moron. I can barely figure out my cell phone. So when I die, it is very unlikely I will be able to figure out how to manipulate these devices to communicate. It would be much easier for me to send a loved one an email from beyond.

OUIJA BOARDS

Okay, any self-respecting paranormal investigator won't even consider using these. Any results are likely caused by over-active imaginations and suggestibility. Second, there is the ideomotor effect to consider, where a subject makes a movement unconsciously. I included the Ouija Board here because I believe we need to consider that the gadgets mentioned might be high-tech versions of this parlor game.

It is important to learn how equipment works, to do various experiments with them, and to thoroughly scrutinize any results. We need to check our egos at the door and be able to consider other explanations before we present anything as evidence. As a friend recently said, "When in doubt, throw it out".

I don't have much faith in the Ovilus, especially the phone app. However, there was one experience where I was exploring rooms at the Buffalo Central Terminal. In one of the rooms, I found a jacket. It had been there for some time, since it was covered in dust and debris. While I was wondering who left the jacket there, I met another investigator in the hallway. He turned on his Ovilus phone app and the first two words it generated were "left" and "jacket". Coincidence is not evidence, I know. But it still gave me goose bumps.

GHOSTS IN THE MACHINES

Increasingly, it seems like a lot of people, are becoming unfamiliar with natural sounds from wildlife and buildings as well as those created by our surrounding technology. The other night I was watching a rerun of a certain paranormal TV show and they claimed to capture an EVP that supposedly was the moan of a murdered woman. Well, what I heard was a cat yowl. As a cat person, I know sounds cats make and I am certain it was a cat, not a ghost. This took place in an abandoned building with broken windows and all sorts of other possible access points for cats (and other noisy critters). This was not the first time I heard something entirely different than what the show presented. One "EVP" (which was also audible to them at the time) was of an old woman screaming. I heard a fox. Being the location is near a vast wilderness area teeming with foxes, and I've actually seen foxes near the location, I'm confident that I'm right. On yet another episode, they heard and recorded, "children's" voices. But I heard the yipping of coyotes, a sound I have become quite familiar with from living in a rural area. That episode of their show was also filmed in a rural area and known coyote habitat.

There was a time when kids went camping - real camping - in the great outdoors. They would learn to identify sounds from the native wildlife. People still camp, but increasingly, it's luxury camping: inside an RV or common camp ground and "plugged in" to TV, radios, iPods, handheld electronic games, smart phones, etc. The natural sounds of the night are drowned out. The same can be said in our own habitats. We are so used to having the TV or radio on, or having iTunes running on our computer as we surf the web. We are surrounded by mechanical noise: the hum of the refrigerator, the hot water heater, the furnace, etc. Outside is the drone of traffic or nearby industry. How do we know what the true sounds of our dwelling may be if we can't hear them? Wind can sound like whispers. Rain hitting the roof can sound like footsteps. A loose rain gutter can sound like knocking. Acoustics can be tricky as vents and pipes carry sounds to other rooms.

One time, several years ago, I was staying at my parents' house. They had bought a new refrigerator since my last visit. That night, while in bed, I was awakened by a frightening sound: someone (thing) was breathing above me. It scared me half to death! Turned out it was the new fridge's icemaker. The refrigerator is located in the kitchen - under a register. My bed was also located under a register and the sound carried to right above me.

The very first day I moved into our current home, I heard someone say "Hello" right behind me, in the hall. I figured my husband came home early and I looked out the front door. Nope. I looked around for someone in the front or back yard. No one there. Because I was so busy, I really didn't have time to stress over it. But a few weeks later, we had a repairman installing a new furnace. I was working in the hallway removing old wallpaper. He came to me, looking a bit shaken, and asked if my husband came home. He hadn't, so I asked why. He said he heard someone talking right behind him. Because he looked genuinely scared, (and I really needed the new furnace to be installed) I said it must have been the radio. A month or so later, we had an alarm system installed and once again, one of the workers asked if anyone else was home because he heard someone talking right behind him. So I was beginning to wonder if we had a spectral housemate. Late one night I was awakened to a dog yipping. It sounded like it was in the house, but didn't sound like my dog. I went downstairs to find my dog sleeping soundly. I went back to bed and again, heard a dog's high pitched bark. So I went back downstairs, where my dog was still asleep. Then I clearly heard my neighbor's voice telling the dog to shush. It turns out we have a culvert in front of the house, and pipes leading to a water main. It acts just like a speaking tube, and if my neighbors are in the right place, their voices carry right into our basement. Because the basement is a big cement rectangle, it acts like a resonance box. Had I not persisted in finding the cause, I could have easily believed my house was haunted.

Today, many people aren't aware of how household appliances function. At one time, more schools offered basic shop classes and people didn't have to rely on calling in plumbers and electricians for minor repairs because they could do it themselves. As for me, I have no clue how to fix most of the technology I use on a daily basis. If this computer goes kaput, I will have to call a tech. If my clothes dryer dies, I will have to call in a repairman. My auto mechanic skills are limited to adding windshield wiper fluid and checking the oil level. (Or more accurately, asking my husband do it, ha ha). My point is when odd things happen in our tech-saturated environment, it's ridiculous to conclude they are paranormal without taking time to analyze and better understand our surroundings.

Technology is all around us, firmly entrenched in our daily lives. We tend to forget that it is prone to glitches. Lights flickering most likely are due to a wiring issue. It's a good idea to call an electrician, instead of an exorcist. TVs and radios have alarms or pre-programmed settings that sometimes inadvertently get set and cause the device to seem like it has a mind of its own when it turns on or off by itself. Older TV remotes (like those still found in some hotels) operate on radio frequencies, so if a TV turns on or off in your hotel room, it doesn't necessarily mean it's haunted. People don't take the time to understand how their cameras work and what causes common artifacts like lens flares, orbs, and light streaks. Pretty much everyone has a cell phone these days. They also come with quirks. Sometimes they call or text programmed contacts "by themselves". While this is a common glitch (it happened with one of my first cell phones) which can occur for different reasons, there are people who still jump to the conclusion a ghost is involved.

Then there is a byproduct of some of our technology: electromagnetic fields. As I've discussed before, there are studies suggesting that EMFs can cause Experience Inducing Fields, which can produce auditory, visual and tactile hallucinations, and even the feeling of a "presence". Taking this into consideration, the United States is the largest consumer of energy. Residential use has now surpassed industrial and business in usage. The average home uses over 25 electric appliances.

I've talked with many paranormal investigators who notice that they seem to get more reports of claims during the winter. Again, there are natural explanations for many of them. Some stem from being cooped up in an enclosed space with the furnace running more often. Carbon monoxide can build up, which is known to create hallucinations and "unexplained" illnesses. This can also be due to toxins from mold or household chemicals circulating. Because of the temperature variance between the interior of the house and the cold outside, air currents can be created and misinterpreted. Also, building materials can contract and expand with the difference in heat and humidity, creating popping or knocking sounds. Animals are seeking warmth from the cold and your walls and attic are very inviting to them. Not only can this explain odd noises, it can also be why Fido is suddenly acting funny and barking or staring at "nothing". Odors trapped in porous materials, such as wood, can be released with heat. Therefore, phantom perfume or the smell of cigars does not mean there is a ghost hanging out.

So when lights flicker or a noise that seems out of place is heard, it doesn't do any good for either clients or investigators to jump to the conclusion that something paranormal is going on. Before we look for answers about the supernatural realm, we should strive to have a better understanding of the natural one first.

> During one investigation, we were in an old building in a historic business district. While we were doing an EVP session on the fourth floor, I heard voices coming from a room behind us. I thought for sure the caretaker left his TV on, which was located right below that room on the third floor. So two of us went to check it out. While I had my ear to the ground, we suddenly heard someone running down the hall right above us, towards a storage room. The two members stationed at the monitor, as well as our cameras, confirmed no one was in that hallway.

PARAPYSCHOLOGY

The term "science-based" has become a popular way many paranormal teams described themselves. They want to set themselves apart from metaphysical teams. However, it is important to understand just because a team flaunts a bunch of gadgets and gear, it doesn't necessarily mean they are truly science-based. As discussed before, the best equipment is utterly useless if it is not used properly or if the data it generates is misunderstood. Furthermore, unless proper protocols and controls are in place, any data gathered cannot be deemed trustworthy. One of the biggest complaints from skeptics and scientists is that many of these teams fail to adhere to scientific principles. One principle that is often ignored in ghost hunting is Occam's

Razor, which states that the simpler hypothesis, meaning one that uses the least assumptions, is the correct one. Many ghost hunters I meet do not have the college degrees or credentials to accurately call themselves scientists (at least not in a professional or academic capacity). But I believe using the term "science **based**" is acceptable – as long as teams actually apply scientific methodology during the entire investigation process.

Some investigators are loosely applying the term "parapsychologist" to give themselves more credibility. (It does sound much more brainy than "ghost hunter"). However, in general, *valid* parapsychologists have advanced degrees in sciences such as psychology, physics or anthropology. For example, the late Dr. William Roll received a BA from Berkley in psychology and philosophy and went to Oxford where he received a Master of Letters (also known as a Masters in Research) in Parapsychology and later a PhD in parapsychology from Lund University. Dr. Barry Taff received his doctorate in psychophysiology with a minor in biomedical engineering.

The last accredited degree in parapsychology (at least that I am aware of) was awarded in US in 1980s. To be accredited, the curriculum has to meet certain standards and requirements as set by the state board of education before it is approved. The general scope of research includes: telepathy, precognition, clairvoyance, psychokinesis, near-death experiences, reincarnation, and apparitional experiences.

The Society for Psychical Research was founded in London in 1882. Not coincidentally, the Spiritualist Movement was in full swing in Europe and America during this time. Early membership included philosophers, scholars, and scientists. Telepathy, hypnotism, apparitions, haunts and physical aspects of Spiritualism like materialism. Soon afterward, The **American** Society for Psychical Research was founded in 1885 in New York City. It was largely supported by psychologist William James.

In 1911 Stanford University became the first academic institution in the US to study ESP and psychokinesis in a lab setting. It was headed by psychologist John Edgar Coover. In 1930 Duke University started studies of ESP and PK in the lab under psychologist William McDougall, with psychologists Joseph Rhine and Louisa Rhine. Eventually other accredited institutions conducted parapsychological research including Berkley, UCLA and Princeton. JB Rhine later founded The Parapsychological Association in North Carolina in 1957. The aim was to advance parapsychology as a science and to integrate findings with other branches of science. In 1969 under anthropologist Margret Mead, the Parapsychological Association became affiliated with the American Association for the advancement of Science.

In the 1970s other organizations formed and the scope of research expanded into altered states of consciousness. Private think tanks and even the U.S. Government were also studying the certain phenomena. Physicist Russell Trug coined the term "remote viewing", which is associated with the "Project Stargate".

Parapsychology always has, and continues to, receive criticism by mainstream science because extraordinary claims demand extraordinary evidence. So far, this demand has not been adequately met. The body of evidence to date is poor (including fraud) and not adequately controlled. In most cases, no conclusive results have been produced. Some critics regard the methods used as pseudoscientific. However, respected scientists, including Carl Sagan and Brian Josephson (noted physicist who won the Nobel Prize in Physics for his work in superconductivity) have said there are some claims that have at least some experimental support and deserve further study. These include claims that people can psychically affect random number generators in computers, telepathy, in which people under mild sensory deprivation can receive thoughts or images projected at them, and precognition.

There is currently ongoing research being conducted by credible scientists. For example, Cornell University's professor of psychology emeritus Daryl Bem has conducted experiments testing the ability of precognition. The results suggest that subjects tested at 53.1% - slightly above chance. It sounds insignificant, but it is larger than the odds a casino has over a player at the roulette table.

But at the end of the day, how does parapsychology affect the average paranormal investigation? In regard to ghost hunting, there has to be more substantial and consistent results of these studies in order to be applied. You can't prove one unknown (ghosts) with another unknown (psi). This is why I have problems with some parapsychologists using psychics when researching hauntings. But, there are some aspects of parapsychology that can help explain some seemingly paranormal experiences. For example, psychokenisis if proven, could explain objects being thrown, or people being slapped by unseen "entities". So I believe these studies are valuable and hope they will one day unlock some mysteries associated with ghosts.

CHAPTER 3: PEERING INTO CREEPY CORNERS: OUT IN THE FIELD

As I've said before, some people involved in this field say there is no "right way" to investigate and I agree to some extent. There is no official consensus or regulation on paranormal investigating. However, I strongly feel that anything that can potentially mislead a client and needlessly create more fear is not the right way to investigate. There have been studies and experiments on various techniques and equipment used in paranormal investigation that have determined they are unreliable. If one is truly interested in helping clients and furthering paranormal research, they will avoid using them in their investigations.

PARANORMAL "EXPERTS"

Am I a paranormal investigation "expert"? Nope. But technically, neither is anyone else! To date, in the US, there is no accredited training or certification that qualifies anyone as an "expert" or "professional" ghost hunter or paranormal investigator. There is no formal body which regulates paranormal investigators or which would protect clients from incompetent or fraudulent investigators. As a former educator, I am all for taking seminars and classes from others in the field (even for a fee) if I feel they can present information that will help me with research. But if they promise a certification in the end, in this field, all that means is you took a class from a person who has as much formal qualifications as you do: **none**. I'm not saying don't take the class, I'm just saying be aware it won't make you a "certified paranormal investigator", or "certified ghost hunter".

Experience is obviously important, but alone is not much of a qualification. For example, somebody could be investigating for 20 years, but if they are not familiar with how their basic equipment works and therefore present false positives as "evidence" then they aren't much of an expert, in my opinion. Writing a book or being on a TV show does not necessarily make one an expert. There are quite a few shows in which investigators use bad protocol, as well as use ineffective (but flashy!) equipment and again, present false positives as "evidence".

Conversely, people can educate themselves with a mountain of resources, but paranormal research requires field experience to learn how to use equipment for that purpose, how to discern what you might perceive on an investigation and how to review and analyze the data you gather. Misperception and misidentification is very common, and the more a person becomes experienced in various locations and situations, the less this will occur.

Because this field is based on speculation and theory, it is constantly evolving as we learn from those who test and review equipment and develop protocols to reduce contamination and false positives. It also requires investigators to be able to separate their ego from their "evidence" and be open to alternative explanations. I have made a lot of mistakes in my quest to find answers, and I am certain to make a lot more. I have had to dismiss some of my own personal experiences that at one time I was convinced were true paranormal events. I have also had to toss out equipment that has been proven unreliable and ineffective in research. But I have learned from those mistakes and am now able to provide a possible explanation for similar claims.

I strongly believe it is unethical for paranormal investigators/groups to charge for their "services". Again, what formal qualifications do they have to justify taking money from people? The existence of ghosts has yet to be proven. There is not even a uniform consensus of what ghosts might be. There are a few theories: the disembodied consciousness of a deceased person, psychic imprints from living people, residual energy imprinted on the atmosphere, non-human entities, etc. So how can someone claim to be able to tell clients they have a ghost, and even more disturbing, can "remove" the ghost for them? **They can't**. No one using objective and observable methods, can. Those who base their evidence on purely subjective methods like psychics, are doing a disservice. I will discuss such methods, and why they are not reliable, later.

I believe the label "Paranormal Investigator" comes with some responsibility, especially if dealing directly with clients. It entails learning about physiological and environmental factors that can contribute to claims, as well as learning about equipment and how they work and how to identify video or audio artifacts. Those who just want to investigate for the thrill or to "find ghosts" are not contributing to any research. I consider them "enthusiasts" but not investigators.

Are there people I consider experts in this field? Sure. But I am wary of those who promote themselves – especially for a fee - as such.

ABSOLUTELY – NOT

One of the problems I see with many paranormal TV shows, books and paranormal investigators, is that they speak in absolutes. Meaning, they assert beliefs that have little or no evidence, as facts. Many of these statements have been repeated so often that they are have become ingrained in popular culture. Here's some common examples:

1. *A "cold spot" means a ghost is present.* Well, not necessarily. There are rational causes to consider first. A change in humidity can make one feel cold. Fear, such as hearing an unexpected noise (especially in a suggestible state) will give a person "chills". EMFs can cause tactile hallucinations, which are often described as a cold sensation. Then there is the

temperature variance between the outside and inside of a building which can cause drafts. For example, in the winter, warm air is forced out of the top of a building and creates a suction of cold air through the bottom (such as a cellar). The reverse happens in the summer. This is called the Stack Effect (as in a chimney stack) and creates air currents within a building. Many times people will suddenly feel cold during an EVP session. This can be caused by your blood pressure dropping from sitting still for while.

2. *Ghosts can manipulate electromagnetic fields.* Since we don't know if ghosts exist, or what exactly they are made of, or what they are capable of doing, this is pure speculation. Unfortunately, it is fueled by some who do not recognize various sources of EMFs, how to properly use EMF meters or what environmental factors affect EMF meters.

3. *Ghosts stay around because of unresolved issues in life.* Maybe. But we really don't have any proof of why ghosts hang around. This idea gained popularity during the Middle Ages when scholars on both sides of the Reformation debate were trying to explain the nature and intent of ghosts.

4. *Cemeteries are haunted, especially at night.* There is no evidence to support graveyards are more haunted than other locations. This belief has been instilled by centuries of folklore. In Western culture, this idea may have originated in Ancient Greece, where the earliest ghost stories depicted the dead as ambivalent towards the living and basically hung out

by their tombs, moaning, so people didn't venture near at night.

5. *Ghosts are more active at night.* There is no evidence to support this. In investigating, I hear just as many claims that occur during the daytime. This belief probably relates to the large number of experiences that are actually products of sleep paralysis and hypnagogic hallucinations. Other things to consider: during the night, our environment tends to be dark which increases the chances for visual misperception. Also our surrounding environment tends to be quieter at night, so we notice noises that we didn't during the day and can misinterpret them, especially if we are awakened, or are drifting off to sleep.

6. *Children and animals are more "sensitive" to ghosts.* Maybe, but there is nothing to substantiate this. This romantic notion became popular in Victorian lore. But there are possible explanations of these reports, especially involving animals. If people are affected by EMFs, it certainly is plausible animals are also susceptible to the same effects, perhaps even more so. In addition, how many times have you heard, "My dog refused to go in the basement.... he'd start down the stairs and run back up". Fuse boxes, which can give off high EMFs are often located in cellars. In addition, cellars act as resonant boxes, which can amplify sound waves including infrasound. Since animals have more acute hearing, infrasound, which can cause seemingly paranormal experiences in humans, can affect animals. Also a dog or cat staring

at a wall or becoming agitated "for no reason" may indeed indicate a presence - of living critters.

7. *Ghosts will haunt if they weren't given a proper burial or their grave is disturbed.* Perhaps, but no one knows this for sure. This belief was popular in the early Middle Ages, again as part of religious debates about the afterlife. It could be argued that from a psychological standpoint, the idea that our final wishes are not carried out, or our resting place will be violated, makes us uneasy.

8. *Doing renovations on a building will disturb ghosts.* Some people have reported such a connection, but then again, many have reported activity where no remodeling has been done. I think this notion is influenced by the stories of "house spirits" found in cultures around the world. A common theme is if these spirits are somehow disturbed by the family, they will turn on them and cause mischief in the house.

9. *Ghosts can only turn on lights, speak into recorders or manifest if they have enough "energy" to do so.* Again, we don't know what ghosts, if they exist, are made up of, how or how they interact with the environment, so this is speculation.

10. *Ghosts drain batteries so they can manifest.* Maybe they do, but other likely causes of battery drain include cold temperatures (in alkaline batteries), change in temperature that might cause

condensation in the equipment, or the equipment has a defect.

11. *Ghosts are "lost" and need help "crossing over"*. At this point, no one knows this to be a fact. This belief may be traced back to religious ideology during the Reformation. Catholics maintained souls go to Purgatory to await their ultimate fate on Judgment Day. Catholic teachings also encouraged the faithful to pray for their loved ones' salvation - the more prayers said for a soul increased their odds of going to Heaven. The Protestants, on the other hand, rejected the idea of Purgatory and believed when one died, the soul went directly either to Heaven or Hell. That meant every spirit encountered had to be demonic. This did not sit well with some who clung to the old Catholic ideas and reported visits from their dead loved ones. Some scholars offered compromises, such as surmising there was a short grace period where the deceased might be earth bound. Others speculated that since there was no Purgatory, some ghosts may somehow become "lost" and unable to find their way to whichever final destination awaited them.

12. *Unwanted ghosts can be commanded to leave.* Again, this is based on speculation. I have heard accounts of ghosts supposedly leaving when asked to do so. I have also heard accounts that this just made the activity worse. Whether these situations actually had more to do with psychology than ghosts, is up for debate.

13. *A building will be haunted if someone died in it or on the property.* If this is really the case, pretty much every house would be haunted! Unlike modern times, it used to be more common for people to die at home than in hospitals. I think this notion could be related to the common belief found in many cultures, where the deceased remain with their family as an active part of the household.

14. *Abandoned prisons and hospitals are more haunted than other locations because of all the energy trapped there from strong emotions by many people over the years.* Maybe, but again, there is nothing to substantiate this. However, there are environmental factors of why people may report experiences in such locations. First, these buildings are empty and are made of concrete, which conduct and amplify sounds, including infrasound. Secondly, many of these buildings aren't secure and are subject to the elements. Wind can sound like voices. Dripping water can sound like footsteps. Animal activities are extremely likely (and sometimes include vagrant humans). Many of these places do not have electricity, so the building has very little light, which is an invitation for misperception. Certain decaying or even vibrating metals often found in these places can affect EMF detectors.

15. *99% of orbs can be explained as dust, but there is still 1% that are paranormal.* Really? Is there some top secret international data base of every orb photo and video ever taken that can back up these statistics? No, there isn't. But it sounds more

scientific. There simply is no evidence that orbs are anything paranormal.

Responsible paranormal investigators should be careful about speaking in absolutes. If our goal is to help people and find valid answers about the paranormal, we should not be promoting unsubstantiated claims.

One question I get asked a LOT is, "Have you ever been scared during an investigation?" Yes, I have. But so far, it's been because of living entities. One was a skunk, who got way too close for comfort. Another was a creepy guy prowling the location and peering in the windows at us. But I admit, I have been startled a couple times by things that I couldn't explain. During the set up of one investigation we heard distinct and loud knocking on a door just a few feet away from me. I nearly jumped out of my skin! There were only three of us in the entire building and we were all standing together. The door had an opaque window, and there was no movement inside. We immediately opened the door, and found only an empty room, with no other access.

HOW TO FIND A LEGITIMATE PARANORMAL TEAM

So you think you might be experiencing paranormal activity. You want some validation that you're not going nuts and an explanation for some odd things that are happening. You might even be frightened to the point you're uncomfortable in your own home or business.   Or maybe you want to become an investigator yourself. How do you find a reputable group?

I'll be honest: it's a crapshoot. Unfortunately, there are a lot of teams in the field who claim they are in it to help people when in reality they are in it for the "thrill" and to get attention for themselves in a "fringe" field. It takes some research on your part to find someone reliable who will help you find answers that will give you some peace of mind.

AVOID TEAMS WHO:

Charge for services. This field is based on theory and speculation only. At this point, investigators are just gathering data. As I mentioned before and will again, there is no accredited training or certification for ghost hunting, so many in the field feel it is unethical to charge for an unsubstantiated opinion.

Claim they are "certified": See above. If they claim they are certified, they were either scammed or are trying to scam you. All it means is they took a seminar from someone who doesn't have any more formal credentials than you or I.

Claim they can certify a place as "haunted". No one has proven ghosts exist, let alone what they are or how they behave. There are diverse theories out there - none proven - as to what makes a haunting: spirits of the dead, residual energy, time slips, psi activity, etc. If you want a certified haunted location, go to an office supply store and make yourself a certificate. It carries the same validity.

Use psychics in investigations: In today's search engine world, there is just no way to trust that any "hits" are genuine. Also, a false hit, generated from a psychic's overactive imagination, can create unfounded fear. It makes for good theatrics on TV, but if you truly want answers, skip this sideshow.

Post photos of orbs, streaks of light, or mists as "evidence": Any sincere investigator will have done their homework on how cameras work and what causes these common photo/video artifacts. So groups who post such are either ignorant or are trying to fool people with false evidence.

Claim they get a lot of evidence: Most seasoned investigators will tell you valid evidence, captured using strict protocols in a controlled environment, is rare. So either these groups are misidentifying false positives or they are being untruthful.

Claim they can "cleanse" a location: No one can back such claims with any proof. In fact, there are many anecdotal claims where such attempts made things worse for the client. So in my opinion, there are only two types of people qualified to handle such cases: medical professionals or trained clergy who consult with psychologists.

Who "name drop": Just because someone met or got pictures taken with TV paranormal investigators does not make them a better investigator. (I have a few such pictures and it doesn't make me special, trust me). And with bad protocols and misidentifying obvious false positives being shown on many of the shows, it's not something I'd advertise. Also, just because a group is part of a team "family" that is profiled on TV does not guarantee anything. Such team families are huge and therefore hard to monitor and manage individual groups or members.

Who pad their "stats": Experience is important, no doubt. But it doesn't necessarily guarantee a better investigator. For example, if someone has been investigating for over a decade and they still present light streaks due from long exposure as evidence, that experience is pretty much null and void.

Other things to consider: Don't be afraid to do a background check on members or ask for a criminal screen. You want to be sure that who you are inviting into your space and around your family and possessions, is trustworthy.

LOOK FOR TEAMS WHO:

Look for logical and natural explanations for claims first. We cannot identify and analyze valid paranormal experiences if we don't rule out all other explanations first. Sometimes, it's a safety issue. High EMFs, toxic molds, and carbon monoxide levels in a home can not only cause people to have seemly paranormal experiences, but can be dangerous.

Use objective means of collecting data: Anyone can walk in and say they feel a presence or an "energy". Doesn't mean it's there. But when there is other measurable data, through pictures, or audio or EMF readings to back it up, then you have something to properly analyze.

Are very selective about what they will consider and post as evidence: Quality over quantity. Who do you think might be more reliable in finding valid reasons for claims? A group who has 100 dubious pictures that can be easily explained or a group with one picture that no one has been able to debunk?

Do not make unsubstantiated claims or promises: As mentioned before, this field is based solely on speculation and theory. There are no absolute facts or answers at this point, so no one can guarantee any conclusive outcome. Valid investigators collect data, offer their opinion on their findings and advise clients with possible solutions.

Who respect your privacy and will keep your case confidential: Investigators should be more concerned about assisting their clients than their own egos.

Who tell you what to expect from them during and after the investigation: It's your space, and you are entitled to know what the process of an investigation will entail.

Who invite you to participate in the investigation: Some teams ask clients to leave the location altogether and it may be for honest reasons: to prevent noise contamination, etc. However, it is your space and you have every right to be there. A good team will teach you protocols to follow so you won't impede the investigation.

Who are happy to answer your questions: Valid teams value educating the general public about the paranormal, as well as the equipment and techniques they use for investigating.

Who are easily accessible by phone or email: This is self-explanatory. If they are hard to contact, they might not be the most reliable people for your investigation.

Remember, you are the client and it's your space. If investigators show up who act unprofessional or if you feel uncomfortable with them, ask them to leave. You have more to fear from the living than the dead.

PARANORMAL INVESTIGATING: THE BASICS

So you've decided you want to go from watching paranormal investigations on TV to venturing out into dark, creepy locations with cool gadgets in hand. Here is some basic info to get you started.

BEFORE YOU GO

Safety first. Never go to a location alone, even if you are familiar with the place. Always use the buddy system. This is for two reasons: one being safety and the other is if something paranormal happens you will have a witness to verify it. Otherwise it's just another story. Always bring a cell phone (make sure it is turned OFF during the investigation) and a first aid kit. Some places you may want to investigate might not have power or are in disrepair. Wandering around in the dark in dangerous conditions is a recipe for somebody getting seriously hurt. Also, in some large abandoned provide plenty of hiding places for sketchy people who might not be too happy that you're there. There is a certain TV show where the cast brags they get locked in. This attempt at bravado is promoting unsafe situations and is just plain stupid. They claim it is to decrease the chance of contaminating their investigation, but following sound protocols can reduce contamination. Besides, if there is someone already hiding out in the building, or there is animal activity it really doesn't matter if they're locked in, now does it?

Always get permission, whether the property seems to be in use or not. An old cemetery or an abandoned warehouse is really enticing for ghost hunters. But going there without permission is still trespassing and illegal. Getting busted not only creates a mark on your record, but it reflects badly on the paranormal community. Plus, it can be dangerous because there are not-so-nice people who also like to use such areas for drug deals, prostitution and other illegal activities who won't like you intruding.

Even if you get permission, always carry your ID. If a police patrol shows up, they will likely ask you to present it. If you don't have it with you, there could be issues that you don't want to deal with. Telling them, "I'm with XYZ Ghost Hunters" isn't going to cut it.

Even though there are no "professional" ghost hunters, because you are dealing with the public, you should act in a professional manner. Wearing tee-shirts with nifty team logos doesn't necessarily make you "professional". When you're dealing with clients, be respectful to them, as well as their property and each other. Put egos and any internal disagreements aside. Do not make claims you cannot back up. You cannot prove, nor "certify" a place is haunted. You might be able to present evidence that something paranormal is going on, but that is it. It is very irresponsible to claim you can "cleanse" a place from ghosts or energy. There is no proof at all that this is possible and you may make things worse for a client. Finally, don't claim you can "help" a ghost. Again, there is no proof that anyone can, and claiming such is nothing more than an ego trip. Plus, if there are spirits around, it is quite disrespectful to make promises you can't keep.

Be aware there are emotionally and mentally unbalanced people out there. If a client seems too eager for you to prove they have a ghost, acts like they are "on something" or if the situation just doesn't feel right, walk away. Unfortunately, there are cases where attention-hungry clients deliberately manufacture evidence or some clients are outright delusional.

BASIC EQUIPMENT

Common sense tops the list. If you are the type to get freaked out over every bump or squeak you hear, you might want to find something else to do with your free time. Remember, the vast majority of claims have natural causes. So if you hear banging in a building it is more likely due to wind, animals, or vibrations than it is ghosts. Be aware of weather conditions and your surroundings. If you hear "whispering" and it's either windy or raining out, it's very likely you're not hearing a ghost. Be aware of conditions that cause drafts and remember that air is not static; it is in constant motion. So even if you're not standing directly in front of an open window, air currents can gust past you. Doesn't mean it's a ghost.

Bring a notebook and pencil. If you experience something that seems anomalous, write down the time and location so you can cross reference it with your audio or video, or find out what other team members were doing at that time. I remember one investigation where we were asking if anyone was there, could they knock for us. Then we heard knocking! But guess what? We found out other investigators were on the floor above us doing "shave and a haircut" knocks at that time.

Flashlights are important. I am not a fan of investigating in total darkness. It really isn't necessary, as there's no evidence ghosts like the dark more than the light, and there is physiological evidence that doing so makes you more prone to visual misperceptions and capturing false positives on video. Again, there may be locations without power, so getting around and investigating safely requires flashlights. Also, in EVP sessions, it's good to know where everyone is and see if they shift or move, then you can "tag it" so you don't misinterpret that sound in review.

Voice recorders might be the favorite tool of paranormal researchers. If you are really serious about getting into paranormal investigating, spend your money here. Buying cheaper, low-end recorders is a waste of time and money. I will discuss recorders in more detail later, but you must know that low-end recorders produce false-positives because of poor frequency response and low sample rates. So ambient noises can sound like words or phrases. Also, low-end recorders do not have good shielding against radio frequencies, so your ghost might really be a radio broadcast.

CREEPY CORNERS

Every ghost hunting show I've seen has investigators using EMF detectors. EMF detectors detect electromagnetic fields and fluctuations in those fields and that's all. They do not detect ghosts. A good and cheap EMF meter to detect natural EMFs is a compass. Again, if you want a "real" EMF meter, save your money and pay for a higher-end tri-axis one, like a Mel Meter or a TriField. Don't waste your money on a cheap, but flashy one (like I did a few years back). Learn how to use your EMF meter, as well as what environmental factors can affect it, before you bring it on an investigation.

Bring a bubble level. You can get these at any hardware store. Many times you might hear claims where people feel disoriented or even like them are being pushed by unseen hands. Uneven floors and stairs can create this effect. Add complete darkness, which also creates a sense of disorientation, and suddenly you have reports of a mean ghost that pushes people. I don't think it's a coincidence that old buildings have reps for being haunted, since it's common with them to find high EMFs from old wiring and uneven floors.

Bring masking tape and trigger objects. If there are claims where things move on their own, bring an object, like a toy, candy, cards, (whatever might be relevant to the claims or history) and some masking tape. Place the object, and tape a square around it. If the object moves out of the square, you might have some paranormal activity going on. But for the love of all that is good and decent, do NOT use a ball as a trigger object. Vibrations, air gusts, gravity (uneven floors) can easily make a ball move, so it's not the most convincing evidence.

Cameras. If you're just starting out, any camera will do. But I advise investing in a good quality camera to reduce false positives. There is a lot of buzz about full-spectrum and infrared cameras. These are neat, but also useless if you don't have a well-lit control shot from a regular camera to use as a reference. Again, learn how your camera works. Learn about low light conditions, and various exposures and how they cause light streaks, shadows, "see-through" images, etc. Invest in a tripod to reduce false positives. If you become serious about investigating, save up for at least one good video camera, not just in hope of catching an apparition, but rather for crucial cross reference of anomalous photos and audio to rule out natural causes.

Bring extra batteries for your equipment. Make sure you fully charge rechargeable batteries and use fresh batteries each time. There is a theory about entities draining batteries. Sometimes it's only colder temperatures that do this, so just be prepared.

A battery draining in one piece of equipment isn't enough to convince me there's a ghost around. But during one investigation, during the initial walk-through, my digital camera's batteries conked out. So I replaced them with new batteries. After a few shots, the new batteries died too. Luckily, another investigator had new ones for me to use, and I had no further issues with that camera. But, yet another investigator's video camera died shortly after the first shift. So he replaced the battery with another that he also charged before the investigation (which I witnessed) and within 5 minutes it, too, died. Two cameras acting wonky might be coincidence. But then the DVR shut down as well... and that was the same case where one of the DVR cameras moved on its own. So maybe we weren't alone?

PROTOCOLS

Investigations are a waste of your time if you don't follow some basic protocols in order to eliminate false positives and misidentification. Throughout the investigation, especially during EVP sessions, there should be no whispering. Simply talk at a normal volume. When doing EVP sessions, set your recorder down or on a tripod. This eliminates false positives from you brushing a finger against it or it against your clothes. Start every session by stating the location, the time and who is present. Verbally "tag" every sound, like people shifting, moving their feet, coughs, burps, stomach growls, etc. Save pictures for before or after an EVP session, as you should try to remain as still and quiet as possible.

When taking pictures, try to take "control shots" when you first enter an area. Since you will likely be in low or no light, say "flash" before you take the picture. That way you don't blind your teammates and reduce the chance of them taking a picture with your flash reflecting off of something and causing a false positive. Also, this will alert them to stand still so they don't change position between your consecutive comparison shots. Cut off the camera strap, and tie long hair back to avoid "vortices" showing up in your photos. Also, be mindful of temperature. If it's cold enough to see your breath you can discount any weird ectoplasm or mists that show up in your pictures. Hold your breath when taking pictures, and remember that mist from breath can show up as long as 30 seconds later. And absolutely no smoking allowed. If you have smokers on your team, designate specific break times and areas for them to smoke.

Take shifts. If you have more than two people, you might consider splitting up to best utilize your time. Be sure to position the two or more teams far away from each other as to control noise or light contamination. If you're investigating for 4-6 hours (or more), take into consideration time to unload, set-up, and do an initial sweep beforehand, and then time after to pack up. It's a good idea to have a checklist so you don't leave any equipment behind.

Plan breaks. Bring water and food to snack on during the breaks (not while investigating). It will be distracting for you and others if your tummy keeps growling during EVP sessions. Also some people mistake light-headedness or headaches for something paranormal when it's just low blood sugar or dehydration.

This is obvious, but do not drink alcohol or take drugs before or during the investigation.

Provocation: some TV shows use this for dramatic purposes. First off, there is no way to positively ID ghosts. There is no way of knowing if you're cussing out an evil entity or someone's dearly departed grandma. Plus with provocation, IF negative entities exist and IF one is around, it might cause more problems for the clients after you leave. If you want to increase the chance of activity or interaction, use trigger objects as discussed before or maybe even play period music, if feasible.

When in doubt, get out. Some people don't believe in negative entities, and that's fine because there is no proof they exist. However, there is no proof they *don't* exist, either. If one can accept the possibility of ghosts, I can't understand why they would dismiss the possibility of other non-corporeal entities. Personally, I like to err on the side of caution. If you think there may be something negative, walk away. Do not confront, or threaten, or provoke. This may look cool on TV, but if these things do exist, then you could be opening yourself up to a dangerous situation that isn't easily resolved. Be aware that there are psychological issues that can be mistaken as demonic attacks. Most ghost hunters I know are not trained and licensed in psychology, so they are not qualified to diagnose or rule out such conditions. Better safe than sorry. Keeping the best interest of the client, in mind, refer them to a licensed professional or their clergy in such cases.

Finally, remember you will need a lot of patience for investigating. Be prepared for long nights where absolutely nothing interesting happens. Be prepared to review a lot of video and audio where you catch nothing anomalous, and then find most anomalies will have mundane explanations. Those who claim to get a lot of evidence frequently are either misidentifying false positives or are being dishonest. But being patient and overly analytical with your evidence has a payoff: when you do get that rare catch, it will be much more likely to be authentic and therefore harder to debunk.

ENTHUSIASTS VS. INVESTIGATORS

Recently I was asked the question, "What's the difference between ghost hunting and paranormal investigating?" Technically, nothing. But then again, what's in a name?

I don't mean the actual name of a paranormal team. There are plenty of valid teams with the term "Ghost Hunters" in their title. This has value in marketing for potential clients that want help specifically with hauntings, and not with UFOs or cryptozoology.

To me, the term "ghost hunting" implies that one has made up their mind that: 1. ghosts exist (this has not been proven) 2. ghosts are the cause of the claims (there is no way to determine this) and 3. one can "catch" evidence of a ghost (again, there is no proof of this). Unfortunately, these people are prone to either misconstrue or manipulate their "evidence" to fit their agenda of "catching" a ghost. This is neither valid investigating nor research. It is a disservice to the paranormal field.

Whenever I attend public ghost hunts or events, the majority of people I meet are what I consider enthusiasts. These are people who have a sincere interest in the paranormal, but are more focused on the fun part of exploring creepy buildings and swapping spooky ghost stories. Many are rabid fans of paranormal TV shows, not that there's anything wrong with that, but some fail to recognize what they see is entertainment, and not legitimate investigating. A lot of these people, unfortunately, base their knowledge of paranormal investigating on these shows without making the effort to properly research the equipment and techniques portrayed by the cast members. I have no problem with enthusiasts, (I started out as one) as long as they don't promote themselves as investigators. Because they typically do not recognize false positives, they are likely to cause more harm than good when "ghost hunting" for a client.

I believe an investigator's purpose is to find valid explanations (paranormal or not) for claims, and set the client's mind at ease, not to create more fear. While a lot of paranormal investigators start out as enthusiasts, they eventually put the time and effort into researching common natural explanations of paranormal claims. They also study and practice proper investigative techniques to avoid creating false positives. One folly of many enthusiasts is that they buy gadgets seen on TV without doing any homework on how useful these devises really are in actual investigations. Not only should an investigator know what the gear is actually designed for, they should be familiar with how it works, and what "quirks" it might have, so again, one can rule out false positives. If the data it generates is subjective rather than objective, it is useless. Coincidence is not evidence. Finally, experienced investigators understand that valid evidence is rare. Most investigations yield nothing anomalous at all. And as I mentioned before, most anomalies have natural explanations. Investigators are willing to thoroughly scrutinize their own evidence before presenting it. And, more importantly, they are open to peer review. This field cannot progress if investigators cling to false evidence.

I am often asked what qualifications are necessary to become a paranormal investigator. At this time, there is no accredited certification or training for paranormal investigating. There are plenty of websites and "schools" that will be happy to charge you for their programs, but they have absolutely no credentials to do so and their "certificates" are only worth the paper they are printed on. As I've mentioned before, I am all for education. So I encourage people to take classes or seminars, as long as they understand it doesn't "certify" them for anything. Personally, I think the best way to become an investigator is to find a good team looking for new members. Most reliable teams have a probationary period where they train new members both in and out of the field.

So whether you're a client looking for help with unexplained events, or you want to join a paranormal team, be aware of the differences between enthusiasts and investigators so you find a group that's best for you.

EVIDENCE AND EGO

You just came back from a paranormal investigation. You had a few personal experiences and anxiously review your audio and video for evidence. You come across a series of pictures where a shadow in the corner appears to be growing. Since some of the claims include people seeing anomalous shadows, you have clearly caught paranormal proof, right? So you excitedly show your photos to your group leader. He takes one look and explains that the angle of the shot changed in each picture, therefore making it appear that the shadow grew larger. He advises you to invest in a tripod.

How do you respond?

Do you:

a) accept his assessment and agree with it; lesson learned.
b) conclude he is just jealous of you and post it as evidence anyway.
c) quit the group and find another one that clearly appreciates true paranormal evidence when they see it.

Answers b and c may seem ridiculous, but unfortunately, they happen often in this field. Why? People claim they investigate to find answers, but really, they are in it to find "evidence" and get a big pat on the back for it. Part of the blame belongs to popular paranormal TV shows. When "reality" shows depict investigators catching supposed "evidence" in every single episode, it sets the stage for unrealistic expectations.

Another culprit is paranormal-based businesses, such as ghost tours or ghost hunts. Since people pay to participate, there is some expectation for something paranormal to happen. So the tour guides or owners actually encourage false positives, such as orbs, so that their customers leave happy. I admit when I took a tour in New Orleans nearly a decade ago, I felt like I was Miss Ghost Hunter America since I caught so many orbs on the tour. The tour guides were so impressed they even asked if they could post MY pictures on their website. Obviously, I had some talent as a ghost hunter. Well no, not really, I just had new digital camera that caught airborne particles and moisture. Was I disappointed when I learned that? A little at first, but then I got over it. Life will go on without ghost orbs.

Look around the web and you will find that many paranormal groups are presenting false positives, or even outright hoaxes, as evidence. There are a ton of investigators out there happy to put up crap as evidence to convince them that they are special. They are in it for the attention, not to help people or to contribute to valid research. No wonder mainstream scientists laugh at us. When so many in our community fail to learn how our own equipment functions, or how to identify basic video or audio artifacts, we deserve it.

What's even more frustrating is the walls egos build. Some paranormal enthusiasts whine that skeptics are closed minded. But when investigators refuse to acknowledge or even entertain that there are other explanations for their "evidence" then they are the ones being closed minded. What's worse is some of these people become so emotionally invested in their "evidence" that they will come up with some creative rationalization in attempt to convince others - or themselves. Then there is the drama that sometimes happens when group members disagree on what should be considered as evidence. I like to adhere to the credo of "when in doubt, throw it out". We need to be willing to over-scrutinize our own evidence, because there are vultures circling, waiting to tear it to pieces the second you post it.

CAROLYN DOUGHERTY

Take orbs for example. We, as a community, should be over this discussion by now. But we're not. Why? Some people just want to believe so badly, that they accept unfounded explanations. I can almost forgive them. The people I can't forgive is those who are shown the many articles and books that show orbs are actually dust and other airborne particles and still try to justify that "their" orbs are ghosts. What they fail to see is that even if they are right, there is no technology that conclusively differentiates their "ghost orbs" from dust. So how can one present something as a ghost when it looks exactly like dust? Cognitive bias is a huge, but common, obstacle in this field.

Some investigators raise the question that we can become too logical or skeptical. I agree we need to keep an open mind. But, personally, I doubt any investigator who isn't open to the existence of the paranormal would be out investigating in the first place. Equipment can be costly. Investigators commit chunks of time not just to participate in an investigation, but to the hours of analysis afterward. Because of these investments, it is understandable why we'd want to cling to some sort of payoff in the form of some tenuous proof. But we have to ask ourselves, how does that benefit a client? How does it benefit research in general? It doesn't.

If we want to be honest investigators, we may have to accept that our payoff might not come in the orm of proof at all.

PSYCHICS AND PARANORMAL INVESTIGATING

Some popular paranormal TV shows profile groups who use psychics in paranormal investigating. Most of these psychics excel in nothing more than theatrics, and with the help of production editing (and, as some have alleged, information fed by producers) it appears they indeed get "hits" pertaining to the location. While this might make for entertaining television, I believe it is a detriment to valid paranormal research. There very well might be people out there with real psychic ability but to date no one has been able to show any substantial proof.

I personally believe in psychic ability - to an extent. Scientific studies have shown that psychics test at slightly above chance. But guess what: those same studies showed that NON-psychics also test at slightly above chance. So I think there is some innate ability in all of us. However, I also believe it is limited, unreliable and unpredictable. Therefore it is not a valid tool for credible investigating.

Why do I believe psychic experiences might be possible? I've had several experiences throughout my life that I can't dismiss as coincidence. For example, one night I dreamt that a friend of mine, who I was in touch with maybe every other month or so, was really excited about something and was trying to tell me about it. This is out of character from his usual subdued self. When I woke from the dream I saw it was 4:45 AM, and went back to sleep. When I got up and I checked my email, I saw there was a message from this friend. Instead of his usual short "just checking in" message, it was quite long, as he was describing a concert he attended that night, which he was obviously very excited about. He sent the message at 1:45AM from the west coast - the same time I woke from my dream on the east coast.

There is no way to validate that any information a psychic, medium or sensitive provides comes from psychic ability. We live in a media-saturated, search engine world. It is easy for someone with an agenda to Google a location or local urban legend and get information. Even if psychics are sincere, it would be impossible to tell if the impressions they are getting is from a psychic ability, or if it is a product of cryptnomnesia: hidden memories that seem original to the subject. For example, it is possible for someone to read about a location and consciously forget about it. But later when they hear the stories and claims associated with the place, they can subconsciously recall that information, and mistake it for psychic impressions.

Psychics, like the rest of us, are susceptible to the power of suggestion and over-active imaginations. And, just like everyone else, they are prone to misperception due to environmental and physiological factors. So they are just as likely as we are to misidentify anomalies and mistake false positives as evidence. Again, even if the person does have some ability and is sincere, these factors place doubt on the validity of their claims.

There are also a few who consider themselves psychic who are fantasy prone or need to feed their egos. Their "ability" attracts the attention they are seeking. I have heard horror stories from seasoned investigators who were called after other teams using "psychics" had left the clients more frightened than before. Of course, the psychic "evidence" could not be supported with any measurable data. This kind of "investigating" is irresponsible. Clients generally call investigators for help, not for a "show" that leaves them even more uncomfortable in their own home.

People claiming to have psychic powers and profiting off of people's fear and grief is nothing new. In the 1880's there was a trio of sisters who had successful careers as mediums. The Fox sisters, Leah, Margaret and Kate, are often credited with creating the religious movement of Spiritualism. Margaret and Kate "communicated" with ghosts through "rappings". The older sister Leah managed their careers for many years. Mediums cropped up all over the country. It became a fad to host séances in the parlor of homes. "Ghost photography" and "ectoplasm" were born. Then in 1888, Margaret Fox confessed that their rapping "communications" were hoaxed and even demonstrated the techniques in public:

"That I have been chiefly instrumental in perpetrating the fraud of Spiritualism upon a too-confiding public, most of you doubtless know. The greatest sorrow in my life has been that this is true, and though it has come late in my day, I am now prepared to tell the truth, the whole truth, and nothing but the truth, so help me God! . . I am here tonight as one of the founders of Spiritualism to denounce it as an absolute falsehood from beginning to end, as the flimsiest of superstitions, the most wicked blasphemy known to the world." — Margaretta Fox Kane, quoted in A.B. Davenport, The Death blow to Spiritualism, p. 76. (Also see "New York World," for October 21, 1888; and "New York Herald" and "New York Daily Tribune," for October 22, 1888.)

Many believers in the authenticity of the Fox Sisters will point out that Margaret Fox recanted her confession a year later. However, it is important to note what her situation had become by that time. After her admission, the Fox sisters were harshly criticized and shunned. Their finances quickly dwindled. So it is more than reasonable to conclude that Margaret recanted in order to try to earn income again. But, it didn't work. By the time the three sisters died within the following five years, Leah and Margaret were living dire poverty and were buried in paupers' graves.

Paranormal investigators should understand how many modern so-called psychics operate. Many are masters of a technique called cold reading. Cold reading is not limited to psychics. Magicians, mentalists, motivational speakers, marketers, sellers and (unfortunately con-artists) use cold reading. A skilled cold reader can seemingly tell intimate details about a person that they've never met without any prior information. In reality, the cold reader craftily elicits information from the subject themselves. They also are practiced in reading subtle body language and non-verbal cues, as well as analyzing other information: a person's dress, posture, grooming, speech, age, dialect, etc. Using all this information, the cold reader can make guesses about the subject with a high probability of being correct or close. Based on the subject's reactions, the cold reader will direct the reading to where the focus is placed on "hits", and where "misses" are minimized or even redirected. The goal is for the subject and audience, if there is one, to recall the hits and dismiss the misses. While the cold reader is doing most of the talking, it is the subject that has given the information away. This is a learned, observable technique that takes some talent and skill, but no psychic ability is needed.

I have witnessed this first-hand. I attended gallery reading of a well-known celebrity psychic. Like many other physics, this one made claims to bolster their abilities: they have an accuracy rate of "about 80%" and have a Native American Shaman ancestor for a spirit guide. (I often wonder why spirit guides have to be exotic; you never hear about one who was a boring accountant named Bob). Then the psychic asked subjects for three pieces of information: the deceased's name, their relationship to them, and the age they were when they passed away. That is a lot of information to work with!! With some skill and practice, anyone could come up with reasonable guesses given that data. But when the psychic did get obvious misses and family members said the information was wrong, the psychic tried to "cover" by making comments like, "Oh honey, he tells me you just don't know the other side of the story". I thought it was obscene how the psychic was deflecting the "misses" back onto grieving families. Unfortunately, gallery readings benefit psychics: while in an audience that obviously supports the psychic, people will be less likely to react defensively. Make no mistake: this is a profitable business. This particular psychic, who claimed they used their gift to "help people" also, informed us they charged $500 for phone readings.

There are state and local laws throughout the United States which restrict so-called "fortune telling" and in some districts, it is even banned outright. In New York State, it is a class B misdemeanor to charge for psychic readings without the disclaimer "for entertainment purposes only":

Under New York State law, S 165.35:

A person is guilty of fortune telling when, for a fee or compensation which he directly or indirectly solicits or receives, he claims or pretends to tell fortunes, or holds himself out as being able, by claimed or pretended use of occult powers, to answer questions or give advice on personal matters or to exercise, influence or affect evil spirits or curses; except that this section does not apply to a person who engages in the afore described conduct as part of a show or exhibition solely for the purpose of entertainment or amusement.

If the goal for investigators is to find credible explanations for paranormal claims, it will best be achieved through objective means of collecting data, not parlor games.

THE DEMON DEBATE

The subject of demons can be a highly contentious topic among paranormal investigators. Some don't believe in demons, some do. It is not my purpose here to convince anybody one way or the other. Personally, I was raised in a faith that teaches they exist, but I have not encountered any credible evidence so far that has convinced me. While I cannot say I am 100% certain there are demons, I will say I believe in the *possibility* of their existence.

The very nature of ghosts, as defined as disembodied souls/consciousness of the deceased, brings up the issue of an afterlife. For many people, this has religious connotations. Christianity, Judaism, and Islam have demons in their traditions. This does NOT make demons real. But it does mean there is the probability that some of our clients, as well as some fellow investigators, may believe in the demonic. A 2007 Pew Forum survey revealed 59% of Americans believe in hell. A 2009 Harris Poll revealed 60% of

Americans believe in the devil. While we might not share those beliefs, we can at least respectfully accept that there are those who do. On the flip side, believers need to recognize that there are different traditions concerning demons and ideas vary on how they (if real) work or how they can be exorcized. For example, in some religions, demons are not evil - they are actually agents working for God, testing the righteousness of humans. That is why stating religious beliefs as facts should be avoided.

Critics will claim that there is no scientific proof that demons exist. They're absolutely right. However, there is no proof of ghosts either, and yet here we are walking around with recorders and EMF meters. Some critics claim demons are limited to the realm of myth and folklore. Again, the same argument can be made of ghosts. I personally don't understand how someone can accept the existence of ghosts but be closed to the *possibility* of other non-corporeal entities. Some people are convinced that reported demons are actually angry ghosts: people who were evil in life are evil in death. They very well could be right and various cultures subscribe to this belief, but like demons, there isn't a shred of evidence to back up this theory. In Christian traditions, demons are fallen angels.

There is a common misconception that demons are an invention of, and therefore restricted to, the Bible. This is untrue. Demons, or comparable entities, are found in cultures around the world, and predate Christianity. In some cases, they are not what we define as evil. Some beliefs place demons in judiciary capacity, working for God to punish the unrighteous. The Sumerians believed in non-human evil entities. Among these is *Ilu Limnu*. In Japanese lore, there are stories of the demon *Akuma* and "Oni-Yuri" or Tsuina" which are ceremonies to exorcize demons. Native American lore also includes demons, some of human origin, some not. It is interesting that a modern retelling of *Atahsaia* by Native People describes him as a demon; not an evil spirit, or ghost, or witch. They consciously chose the term demon.

Another common mistake is assuming that investigators who believe in demons will automatically look for them and have preconceived conclusions regarding the demonic during investigations. That is an unfair generalization. Just because some may believe, doesn't mean they see demons in everything. I for one don't go into investigations looking for ghosts or demons; I look for rational answers. I strongly believe that once we identify common explanations for claims, we then can begin to recognize and analyze truly paranormal experiences. Unfortunately, there are groups and investigators out there who do focus on the demonic, and make unverifiable claims that they can "cleanse" a home, etc. (usually for a fee). If demons exist, there is no proof or guarantee that anyone - including Church trained exorcists - can get rid of them. Those who do promise they can help are either ignorant, ego-maniacs, or are outright scamming people. First off, assuming there are no demons involved, these people could end up feeding delusions of a disturbed client. On the other side of the coin, there are anecdotal claims from victims of alleged demonic experiences that their situations grew worse after such attempts.

Today there are popular paranormal TV shows that profile alleged demonic cases. Even well-known demonologists have claimed that demonic cases are extremely rare, and have publicly stated the increase of such shows is irresponsible because they are creating unnecessary fear and cases of misidentification.

As I mentioned before, we need to first find rational, logical explanations for any paranormal claims. That is why responsible demonologists and Catholic Church officials now consult psychologists and medical doctors in suspected cases. In fact, psychological or physiological issues are most often found to be the cause of demonic claims in modern times. Some can argue they were always the cause. People with certain psychological disorders can appear possessed. Those with schizophrenia have trouble discerning what is real. This obviously affects their behavior, emotions and cognitive abilities as well as motives for destructive behavior. Those suffering from psychosis are prone to hallucinations and/or delusions, which are fixed or obsessive beliefs that often have no basis in reality. These people also often suffer from paranoia and drastic personality changes. Dissociative Identity Disorder, (also known as Split Personality) is a disorder that obviously can seem like possession. In fact, one report estimated that 30% of people with Dissociative Identity Disorder claim demons as one or more of their identities.

There is a fairly common sleep disorder that can be mistaken as demonic activity. The phenomena of the "night hag" and *incubi* and *succumbi*, (demons who attack sleeping victims in their bed and assault them physically and sexually) have been found to have a physiological cause. Sleep paralysis is a disorder that has been induced and observed in labs. To the subject, the experience feels very real, but in fact, they are suffering from a severe form of hypnagogic hallucination.

The mind is a powerful thing: there are reported cases where people who, under hypnosis, were told that their hand was burning and they actually developed blisters during the session. So if a person is delusional, they may indeed develop injuries and illness that would seem consistent with their delusion.

There is also suggestibility to consider. For example, people who suspect they might be around something demonic may misidentify simple injuries. What actually is a rash can appear as a bite mark. Scratches that may have been the result of working in a rose garden suddenly are evidence of a demon. We humans are not graceful creatures. We often injure ourselves in our daily lives, and are either unaware of it at the time or are so busy that we quickly forget about it. But when we're *looking* for "evidence", these injuries can become problematic.

Substance abuse has also been attributed to experiences mistaken as "demonic". According to a recent report from the CDC, abuse of common prescription pain killers and antidepressants now surpass the abuse of heroin and cocaine combined. Severe alcoholism in women has also increased. These factors can contribute to hallucinations and delusions. Add suggestibility to a chemically imbalanced mind, and you have a situation where "demons" can manifest.

Another fact investigators should be aware of is that there are documented cases in which demonic claims (and even general hauntings) are used as a cover for physical or sexual abuse within a family. So investigators who are convinced they are dealing with demons in these cases are indirectly contributing to the problem instead of helping the victim of something truly evil.

Perhaps even more disturbingly, there have been severe injuries and even deaths resulting from attempted exorcisms from various religious traditions. (The Catholic Church, thanks to popular culture, is most associated with exorcisms, but there are many religions that conduct them.) Understandably, this dark history creates doubt on claims of demonic possession and exorcisms. But I pose this question: by comparison, how many cases are there where the alleged exorcism was successful?

We don't know. That is why I am hesitant to paint all cases with the same broad brush.

In my opinion, not all "symptoms" of possession, if true, can be explained away by medical issues - at least not yet. For example, there are credible claims of victims knowing extremely personal information about others which they could not possibly have access to. Another common claim about possession is victims being able to hold a conversation - not merely spouting out random words or phrases - in foreign languages unknown to them. This is not to be confused with "speaking in tongues", which usually is meaningless babble that cannot be attributed to language. I'm not saying this indicates there are demons, but it certainly can be considered paranormal.

How does this affect us as paranormal investigators? If you don't believe in demons and you have a client with such concerns, you have two choices: explain to them upfront that you base your investigation solely on scientific data. Or simply don't take the case. For investigators who are open to the possibility of demons, it will benefit both you and the client if you look for logical explanations first. I cannot emphasize that enough! Keep your personal beliefs to yourself. Quite frankly, you could be wrong and spreading misinformation. Creating fear is counter-productive to paranormal research. But there are things you might want to look out for during investigations. Some demonologists warn that entities who can cause *significant* physical harm (more than a shove or slap) might be non-human. Also, those entities who are "chatty" and want to hold your attention might not be of human origin. Demonologists also caution against entities posing as children and loved ones that are trying to interact with you (especially on a location that they wouldn't have had any association with). You have no way to identify that what you're talking to actually once was a child or something else. Mimicking is supposedly a way for a negative entity to keep you engaged, and the alleged danger is that the longer you are interacting with something negative, the more susceptible you become for oppression or even possession. If you suspect a negative entity, walk away. Of course, I must add the disclaimer that this is all based only on anecdotal observations and theological speculation. Obviously, all of these examples may also have a non-paranormal explanation.

So the debate continues. But I do want to emphasize that whether psychological, physiological or supposed demonic causes, most paranormal investigators are ill-equipped to handle such cases. Unless we hold appropriate credentials which enable us to diagnose both physical and psychological conditions, we are not qualified to provide help in these situations. The responsible thing for us to do is refer such clients to a mental health provider, physician, and, if appropriate, their personal clergy.

CHAPTER 4: DON'T CROSS THE STREAMS: ISSUES IN THE PARANORMAL FIELD

When I first became involved with the paranormal community, I possessed an egocentric naiveté that everyone had the same intent as me: to network with fellow paranormal enthusiasts and exchange ideas and opinions in a friendly way. (I can be a pollyanna type of gal). So, I was quite blown away by the harsh reality! The unfriendly seem to outnumber the friendly, or at least, keep them cowering in the shadows, afraid to participate because any input will be torn to shreds by rabid trolls lying in wait. To be fair, I have yet to find ANY topic free of this plague, especially on the internet, where people have adopted the screaming pundit mentality instead of participating in thoughtful, respectful dialogue. Even book club sites I've visited have their share of this school-yard bully drama.

Much of the drama stems from the fact that there are investigators who post their evidence, claiming they want honest opinions. But in reality, they just want affirmations that they caught something paranormal. They get very defensive over rational explanations of their ghosties. On the other side of that, you have cynics who automatically declare anything presented as misidentification or fraud. I also see a lot of hypocrisy. Recently, one investigator who I've seen call people "stupid" for posting orbs and mists as paranormal evidence, went on a rant when his own audio evidence was called into question because of the type of equipment and format he used, which was a valid opinion.   It amazes me that many of those who spend so much time criticizing others are the least able to *take* criticism.   Then there are those who claim they've been bullied, only to turn around and cyber-stalk and slander people. (Yours truly has been a victim of this).

There IS bullying out there. I have had fellow investigators request I remove some people from my friends list on Facebook because I might be found "guilty by association" because they feel their evidence doesn't meet certain standards. Sorry, but no. It's hypocritical to claim we want to help dispel misinformation if we shut out the misinformed or inexperienced.   I've also had people harass some of my Facebook friends just for being fans of certain paranormal TV shows.   And I've had people demand that I unfriend others on my friends list because they had issues with them. I had my fill of such nonsense way back in junior high school.

There is also some staggering arrogance out there, jealousy issues, and rivalry between individuals or even groups.   I have even heard of groups being sabotaged by other groups. In one case, an "anonymous tipster" warned of a group who were stealing from clients.   It turned out it wasn't true: there were no such complaints against this team, but there was a former teammate who was very bitter about being kicked out of the group and wanted to get back at them.

With all these issues, it is no wonder why teams bash each other, why individuals in teams get into conflicts, why so many teams break up, and why a lot of good investigators get burnt out and walk away from the field entirely.

Some in the field have uttered the cry for "paranormal unity".   The idea is that we will all get on board as one big happy family. But the reality is, there are just too many conflicting viewpoints, agendas and bloated egos for this to ever happen. There are people who approach the paranormal from a strictly metaphysical view and there are those who approach from a rigid scientific standpoint. There are those who prey on the grieving and fearful for their own gain. There are those who are in it for research, while others are in it for the excitement and attention.   So the idea is a nice one, but I don't think it will ever happen.

THE UPHILL BATTLE: FIGHTING MISINFORMATION

The more I do investigations and talk to people about paranormal research the more I see a real need for education in this field. Clients, friends, and people in the general public are misinformed, largely from popular media like TV shows and new age books. Some ideas have been presented and repeated enough to have become engrained in public consciousness as "facts". It is important to note, once again, that this field is all theory and speculation at this point.

The really discouraging thing is, many paranormal groups are also misinformed and are going into people's homes and further spreading inaccuracies. I want to make it clear that I recognize I still have a lot to learn myself in this field. It is constantly evolving. However, before I even labeled myself an investigator, I put in a lot of time and effort to educate myself about common techniques and equipment used in paranormal investigation. This is something that too many groups fail to do, as is evident by their obvious lack of understanding of common causes of false positives, or equipment, protocols, etc. It bothers me that these people claim they can help others when they haven't learned the basics of the field first. That is why too many websites are bombarded by lens flares, light streaks from double exposures, and other common camera artifacts as well as ambient noise falsely called EVPs

Our group has participated in a Paranormal Expo. As expected, there were a lot of psychics and tarot card readers. As mentioned before, I don't consider psychics valid tools in paranormal investigations because it is a strictly subjective technique. The discouraging thing for me as a science-based investigator, is that crowds flock to these people. Why? Because they tell them what they want to hear, which is not always the truth. One example of why I can't take psychics seriously: my teammate was trying to get a picture taken with a turtle because of an ongoing inside joke. A so-called pet psychic actually PUSHED him out of the way, stating she had to "read" the turtle immediately. (Personally, all I can think that would be on a turtle's mind is,"I'd like more lettuce".) Such theatrics are unfortunately common in the psychic community and undermines any true ability, if it in fact exists.

There were several paranormal teams present at the expo and many displayed pictures of them with para-tv celebrities, as if this somehow makes them more "credible". I have such pictures myself. I can assure you that paying for an event and standing in line to snap a picture with a TV personality does not make me, or anyone else, a better investigator. Many of these shows portray bad investigating, including poor protocols, misuse of equipment and presenting false positives as evidence, so why would anyone who is serious about paranormal investigating consider this a boost to their credibility? If I get my picture taken with Rachel Ray, it won't make me a better cook. (Although my husband might wish that were true.)

Most teams (ours included) displayed their gear to "prove" they are science-based groups. But using gadgets does not necessarily mean a team is science-based. Teams must a) know how the equipment works, b) what it is designed to measure, c) how to recognize false positives it may generate, and d) properly analyze its data. Since there were useless (or if you prefer, subjective) gadgets on display such as KIIs and Shack Hacks, it is clear that such groups are simply copying what they see on TV and not doing any reliable research on these devices at all. It concerns me that they were using them to present "evidence" to clients, and possibly creating unnecessary fear.

Many of the groups were eager to show off their evidence. I would like to suggest that if you don't want an honest answer, then don't ask. A lot of investigators were closed off to informed opinions about their "evidence". I believe either you are in this field to feed your ego, or you are in it for valid research and the client's best interest. If it's truly the latter, then you will be open to learn from others, even if that means you have to discard evidence or gadgets along the way - just like the rest of us have to do as we are constantly learning and reassessing. It is the only way this field can progress. Clinging to false evidence and useless gadgets is counterproductive and is a disservice to clients who ask for help.

Adding to the ignorance saturating the paranormal community is something much more insidious: fraud.

FRAUGHT WITH FRAUD

We encountered a team at a Paranormal Expo that tried to fool us and other attendees. They presented interesting evidence but then lied about use of controls and protocols to pad their credibility. When asked, they couldn't present evidence of either.

For the record, if you tell me that you had control shots and video to back up your picture of an apparition, but go on to say you somehow lost them, I (and any other person with minimal intelligence) will conclude you are lying. Honest science-based teams recognize that control shots, comparison shots and video are just as important as the picture with the anomaly. Without them, there can be no honest peer review and analysis of the evidence.

There are different categories of frauds. Most commonly, there are groups putting out misinformation unintentionally because of simple ignorance. They have failed to take the time and make the effort to educate themselves in how their equipment works and how to identify false positives. They are so eager to throw "evidence" up on their websites to show off that they don't bother doing their homework. While we all had to start out somewhere, I still mention them here because they are going into homes and businesses presenting false "evidence" and possibly creating more fear for their clients. While it is different from deliberate fraud, it is still counterproductive to paranormal research and insulting to the teams who work hard to dispel common misconceptions.

In my opinion, it is fraudulent for teams to charge for their services. Since there is no accredited certification or credentials for paranormal investigating, what authority do these people have to charge for something based on nothing but speculation? The existence of ghosts has yet to be proven. So teams that say they can "validate" a haunting or can "cleanse" a place of ghosts or other entities cannot substantiate these claims. Clients call us for help and we should be grateful to them that they are providing us an opportunity to do our research.

There are also those who charge for Spirit Box sessions and EVP sessions. Again, there is no conclusive proof that the voices captured with these techniques are ghosts. Also, people should beware that these techniques can be easily manipulated for hoaxing.

Then there are the groups who flat-out manipulate and manufacture evidence. This is the most overt type of fraud. The internet is rife with fake ghost photos. With the advent of Photoshop and ghost photo apps on smart phones, it takes very little effort to create these. It does take some effort to spot the fakes. At one time, we could rely on the EXIF data to clue us in. Unfortunately, that is no longer the case. Thanks to common video editing software, there are also a lot of fake ghost videos being circulated on the web. YouTube has a host of these. Unfortunately, I no longer trust any photo or video unless I was there when it was taken. Some of these are done by pranksters who really have no interest in the paranormal. But, there are quite a few done by paranormal groups as well. These people are pathetic. One group, who apparently were going to do a TV show, even put out a fake missing persons report on a child who "disappeared" during one of their "investigations". This exploits real families with missing children.

What's even more interesting is that sometimes the fraud is committed by the clients! One such example can be found on YouTube: Go to YouTube.com and search for "The Case of the Flying Nut". Some people just want a good story to tell to get some attention and impress their friends. It is also important to remember that in some cases, clients have claimed they have paranormal activity in order to cover up abuse.

There are several websites out there that are addressing fraud in the paranormal. For the most part, this is a good thing for the paranormal community. Since there is no regulatory body overseeing paranormal groups, we have to police ourselves and call out deliberate fraud when we see it.

Those of us who are interested in valid paranormal research are facing an uphill battle. But, thankfully, many of us ARE facing it. We are actively using education and networking to counteract the misinformation and fraud plaguing this field.

FRAUD SQUADS

For the record, I support calling out fraud in the paranormal. Overt, malicious, deliberate fraud. The parasites who prey on the grieving and fearful, and scam them out of money. Those who use bogus titles and certificates. Those who purposely manufacture fake evidence. Those who make unsubstantiated claims that they cannot back up.

Having said that, I must emphasize there is a difference between the types above and those who make honest mistakes because of inexperience or ignorance. We are ALL still learning in this field!!! As we investigate, conduct experiments and gain experience out in the field, we continually re-evaluate our theories, gear, techniques and protocols. The field is saturated with misinformation perpetuated by TV shows and other popular media, so it's easy to understand how some well-intentioned investigators can be misled.

Lately, I see a disturbing trend of self-appointed "Fraud Squads" attacking paranormal teams. They claim they are calling these teams out to better the field. If they have the backbone to address the team directly in order to educate them, then I can agree. However, some of them are simply posting pictures from the teams and trashing them - WITHOUT the team's knowledge! They do this on their websites, personal Facebook pages or in closed groups. This does not serve any constructive purpose: 1) It doesn't give the team the benefit of the doubt that they simply made an honest mistake, and 2) It doesn't give the team a chance to learn from their mistake and redeem them.

Ironically, some of these Fraud Squaders have been asked to present their credentials of expertise and they fail to do so. (Most likely because they don't have any.) Also, some of them have never even been on an investigation themselves and yet they feel they can second-guess and criticize teams from behind the safety of their keyboards. To me, this is a bit hypocritical. Those of us who actively investigate are capable of making same suppositions. But because we are actually at the location, we also are able to physically validate or dismiss those suppositions. Maybe not in the same night, but possibly on a return investigation.

Because there is no formal governing body in the US that regulates paranormal investigating, these "Paranormal Police" are self-appointed and have no more authority in the field than the teams they are calling out. Many teams do utilize expert opinions from various professions such as photography. For example, there is a professional photographer in my family who has a degree in photography and decades of professional experience in both commercial and industrial photography. I also have close friends who have degrees in photography and graphic arts. But outside of common photographic artifacts or manipulation of images, they admit that unless they were at the location at the time, they can only speculate, but not conclude 100%, what caused an anomalous light source or shadow in a picture.

Sometimes, albeit rarely, there are pictures that might not have an easy explanation. While I believe the overwhelming majority do have natural causes, there are a few that could be of real interest to us as researchers - especially those that were taken with sound protocols to avoid contamination as well as those that have comparison and control shots. So if teams reject second guesses from those who weren't there, it doesn't necessarily mean they are lying or trying to deceive anyone. It may simply mean they don't have answers - yet. As Carl Jung said: "I shall not commit the fashionable stupidity of regarding everything I cannot explain as a fraud".

I am all for education in this field as long as it is done in a constructive manner. That is why I created my blog and why our team produced podcast. But trolling through the internet to target teams and attack them behind their backs is NOT educational. It is counterproductive and only serves to create more negativity and drama.

PARANORMAL PROFITEERING

The popularity of ghost hunting TV shows has brought opportunities for some people to "cash in" on the paranormal. Unfortunately, much of the general public (and even some "investigators") do not recognize that such TV shows favor ratings over reality and editing over evidence. These shows feature poor protocols for investigating, poor analysis of "evidence" and their audiences are being fooled into thinking they are watching valid research. Add investigators with interesting personalities, and you create fans that will rabidly defend these shows, even if techniques or conclusions defy common sense. I've met several of such TV paracelebs, and yes, some seemed really nice and were a lot fun to talk with. But it doesn't mean they are good investigators. It certainly doesn't excuse misleading the audiences with questionable or perhaps even manufactured evidence.

As investigators, we need to recognize entertainment vs. valid investigating and research, and strive to educate others about the distinction. There was a show that initially, I felt was an asset to paranormal research. They ditched the psychics and metaphysics, debunked orbs as dust bunnies and approached investigations from a skeptical standpoint. However, that changed over seasons and now they present "evidence" that they would have tossed out in the first season. They sold out. Many shows that followed did the same.

I have talked to several team founders who have been approached by TV shows. But the producers they talked to made it clear that they wanted more sensational cases, and did not give the investigators control over content or ownership of their own evidence. So they passed on their "big break". From their experiences, it is clear to me that show producers exaggerate, edit, and flat out manufacture claims and evidence in order to create a packaged product that sells. In addition, I know investigators from two different teams who participated in a reality show about ghosts. In their filmed interviews, they presented alternative explanations for claims on the profiled cases - but their segments were never used in the show.

CAROLYN DOUGHERTY

The popularity of TV paracelebs has spawned conferences and events where you can pay to meet or even "investigate" with your favorite paranormal personality. At least some of these events are actually beneficial: some have been set up where part of the profits goes to restoring historical locations. As someone who has volunteered in different historical societies, I'm all for that. Some also provide basic "ghost hunting" seminars. While I can't agree on all the techniques or equipment they discussed, I can say the seminars I have attended at least covered safety, respecting property, and that orbs are not ghosts. But again, just because someone is on TV or the radio, or wrote a book, does not make them an expert, nor does it mean they are presenting valid information. They are there to make some money.

I have been asked why I "hate on" some of the popular paranormal shows. I don't hate them. In fact, I still watch them occasionally and sometimes attend events. But it's frustrating when we're called in by clients wanting answers when they have already done their own "investigating" by blindly copying what they see on TV. The results are usually false positives, and now the clients are sure they have a ghost. During one case, a client who announced he watches the entire ghost hunting shows had used a cheap recorder to do EVP sessions. He proudly played his "EVPs" for us. We heard nothing but sounds commonly produced when one holds the recorder while moving around. However, he had convinced himself that they were demonic voices.   On another case, a client showed me a picture of an "energy vortex", much like those displayed on the TV shows she watched. I explained it was just a bleached- out picture of hair too close to the lens. I explained about the orb zone in pictures and gave her links to examples and articles that she could research for herself. But it was no use.   She wanted to cling to the idea she caught "proof".

As various supposed haunted locations attract interest after being featured on TV, many of them are now charging a hefty fee for groups to investigate. Riding on those coat tails are lesser-known locations that will also let local groups investigate - for a price. Again, there is good and bad in this. I can support historical locations that use the profits towards maintenance and restoration. However, there are cases where someone says their restaurant is haunted and charge gullible groups, not for valid research, but for building their business. Unfortunately, whether on purpose or not, some of these places are perpetuating false evidence as well as unsubstantiated stories. They encourage orbs, bad recordings and information "validated" by psychics. Again, this appeals to paranormal enthusiasts, but is a detriment to legitimate research. It also spreads misinformation, and even fear, to the general pubic.

Our group went to a popular "haunted" location.   This place was featured in a couple of popular TV shows and has been mentioned by many paranormal groups as an active location. After our investigation, I think the most active thing there is imagination. We were able to debunk several of the claims (including experiences featured on the shows) using simple common sense. The owner set up the place for maximum creepiness. There were strategically placed dolls, scarecrows, cut outs and coat racks, so as people navigate in the dark and come upon these unexpectedly, they get startled. There were other props, like wheelchairs and chairs placed in random spots, and fake cockroaches spread throughout the floors. My favorite "prop" was a harmless vase of fake flowers placed in the hallway. Through an infrared camera, the vase is nearly invisible, and the flowers look like a white blob floating above the floor. In addition, many of the stories were just that: stories with no documentation. So some of the most famous "ghosts" of that location are likely only products of fantasy.

This is not to say the place doesn't have paranormal activity. It very well might. But my point is that the owner of the location is using misinformation and false evidence to promote it as legitimately haunted to lure not just enthusiasts, but serious investigators, and then charging a hefty fee for them to investigate. Some may think I am just bitter from a case of "buyer's remorse". Not really. I had already found alternative explanations for a couple of major claims before I set feet there (which were confirmed). But this isn't the first such location I have been to, and what set this one apart was use of props, and the amount of undocumented stories and specious claims supported by paracelebs, but not research.

A lot of major cities have "ghost tours" where you walk around historic neighborhoods and are told ghost stories and claims to back them up. I personally love these tours, because of the history and folklore. However, they also are in it for money, which means they encourage false evidence. On every such tour I've been on, some person will snap a picture, and "catch" an orb. Which isn't surprising when you have groups of 10-20 walking and kicking up dust? They also catch "light anomalies" which again, is not surprising, since they usually take place after dark, and the shutter speed in automatic cameras will slow down and will create long exposure pictures. But the tour guides actually encourage the false notion that these pictures captured something paranormal, therefore spreading misinformation.

Some of these "haunted" locations and ghost tours actually guarantee a paranormal experience. There is absolutely no way anyone can guarantee a genuine experience. Period. Unfortunately, the way some unscrupulous location or tour owners are achieving these impossible results is by promoting false evidence or, in some cases, even rigging the place. Also, some claim to be led by "professional" ghost hunters. I can't say it enough: there's no such thing. But it's a great gimmick to lure unsuspecting tourists.

Once such location is Moss Beach Distillery in California. For many decades, a story of the Blue Lady haunting the location was associated with the place. Over the years, there were claims from many people, including respected parapsychologists that seemed to support a valid haunting. Unfortunately, several years ago the owners decided to rig the building to replicate the claims. Chandeliers are rigged to swing, there are fans to blow ghostly breezes on patrons, and they even have a mirror rigged for a ghostly face to appear. Unfortunately, such manipulation discredits any true experience anyone may have at that location now.

Sometimes locations don't have to use mechanical means to rig a place. All it takes is a good, believable story that has been told and retold so many times it becomes engrained as fact. The Myrtle's Plantation in Louisiana is such a place. The story of Chloe is well-known among paranormal enthusiasts and has been featured on TV shows and in books luring investigators:

Chloe was a house slave with whom the owner was having an affair. One day he caught her eavesdropping and cut off her ear as punishment. She did not want to go back to the fields, so she came up with a desperate plan. She baked a birthday cake for one of the owner's children and laced it with oleander leaves to make the family sick, so that she could nurse them back to health and keep her place in the house. But the plan backfired because she used too much of the leaves and the wife and children died from the poisoned cake. Fearing punishment for her actions, fellow slaves captured Chloe and hung her from a tree in front of the house.

A tragic story and certainly a recipe for ghosts. One problem: apparently, it didn't happen. Paranormal investigator Bobbie Atrisain did some in-depth research into the location. She found there is no record of either a house or field slave named Chloe in the property or slave holding records. Oh, and the inconvenient fact that the wife and children died from yellow fever, not a poisoned cake.

Even when presented with facts, some stories and hoaxes refuse to die. An example is the Amityville Horror. A few careers were built from it, so it's understandable why those who profit from it would want to perpetuate it as fact. Long story short: Butch Defeo, a drug addict who was known to have a contentious relationship with his father, murdered his entire family, including his younger siblings. He is currently rotting in prison. George Lutz bought the house and moved in with his family. The Lutz's claimed they had terrifying encounters with demonic entities in the house. Interestingly, as noted in *Parapsychology: The Controversial Science* by Richard S. Broughton, parapsychologists from two separate organizations who Lutz contacted "for help" didn't find his claims credible nor any indication of paranormal activity. However, they did see a contract to share profits from book rights with Defeo's lawyer's signature on it. Unfortunately, these facts got lost in the ensuing media circus. The media was there to fuel the sensational story, but they were conveniently absent when researchers provided facts contradicting the Lutz's story and even a public admission by the Defeo's lawyer, providing damning evidence that their story was a fabrication. The only thing haunting subsequent owners of the house are gawkers. But today many in the general public still believe the book and subsequent movie was based on real events. But what about a picture of the "Ghost Boy" taken by the famous demonologists Ed and Loraine Warren? Even they admitted their investigation was not scientific. There were investigators, photographers and reporters milling around the house. So in reality, the photo is of an investigator kneeling to set up equipment.

Another problem is that some paranormal investigators or groups are charging clients for their services. This field is all theory and speculation at this point. All we are doing is collecting data and forming an opinion. No one has proven ghosts exist, or even what they might be. Some groups not only charge for investigating, but they also charge for "cleansings". Again, there is no evidence for these unsubstantiated claims. One group even goes so far as to investigate (at a higher fee) if you are in process of purchasing a house so you know if you're future home is haunted or not. Here's the problem: as mentioned before, no proof of ghosts exist. Photos containing light artifacts are not proof of ghosts. EVPs are not proof of ghosts because there are alternative explanations. The problem is the seller

Inducing Fields. (EIFs) Lab studies have shown complex fields affect the human brain, and induce hallucinations and other sensations that can be misperceived as paranormal. These studies indicate that not everyone is susceptible to hallucinating in these fields. Only 20- 30% experienced hallucinations when subjected to these fields. (This supports an observation by Dr. Roll that some people seem more sensitive to these fields than others). In addition, people needed to be subjected to the fields continuously and for some time, before they would experience hallucinations. For now, it appears natural occurring EMFs are too low to induce experiences - on their own. However, when other factors come into play, they might contribute to these experiences.

We live near a fort with its share of paranormal claims, where we frequently walked our dog. One evening, she stopped dead in her tracks, while staring at an empty space in front of the north wall, and started growling. It took some effort to pull her away from "whatever" she was growling at. On our walks she commonly encountered squirrels, bunnies, foxes, woodchucks, other dogs and people, but never reacted like this before. There are all sorts of environmental factors that could contribute to EIFs and infrasound at this location, but why would she be affected by them only once over a 13 year period?

Tectonic Strain Theory has been discussed as a possible source of EIFs. Stress on the rocks from and realtor can lose a sale over false evidence while this group makes money off of it.

Paranormal profiteering has also gone to ridiculous new lows. On Ebay, there have been "certified haunted" dolls and other items for sale, as well as ghosts in a bottle, and *succubi* available for purchase. There are people who charge for Frank's Box sessions. Again, there is no proof at all that ghosts communicate through such devices. In fact, there are plausible explanations for the "messages": pareidolia, phoneme restoration effect, or formant noise, yet some people make money off of it.

Some may argue that if people want to waste their money that's their problem. But it goes deeper than that. Paranormal profiteering is creating misperceptions as well as fear in the general public. It creates a disruption of valid research of the paranormal. The reality is, there are people living in fear because of false information. We still deal with clients who think they have a ghost just because of an orb showed up in their home picture! As investigators we sometimes face an uphill battle when we present logical explanations for claims, yet clients argue, "But I saw this on TV....". As we strive to educate, we are constantly battling the piles of lies put out by people who only care about their egos and wallets, and not the damage they are doing.

I have no problem with people making money off of the current paranormal craze, I just have a problem with those who do it by perpetuating misinformation and the outright manufacturing of "evidence".

SCIENCE AND SENSIBILITY

Not long ago, I got sucked into an online argument with someone who is a hard-core skeptic. The argument concerned whether electromagnetic fields can affect people. I have read studies suggesting they do, he sited studies suggesting they don't. The problem is, all of these studies are inconclusive. So basically, we're still at square one. But then this person decided to attack me on a personal level. He stated my "professional integrity" was in question and I was doing more harm to the field than overt frauds by "forcing pseudoscience on clients".

Those who follow my blog, or who have actually been on investigations with me, know I do not - nor have I ever - presented myself as an expert or a professional in this field. I contend that until we have more substantial facts to work with, no one else really is either. As far as "forcing pseudoscience" onto clients, that is simply untrue. I present clients with possible alternative explanations. It is extremely irresponsible to let good people believe they have ghostly activity when there could be another reasonable cause (backed with compelling data) of what they are experiencing. One example is hypnagogic hallucinations. There is no way to measure and package these phenomena in a way to present to a client. So then, should I neglect to tell a client about this fairly common sleep disorder so they can seek a physician's help, or should I let them go on believing a demon is attacking them at night? As investigators, if we claim we are trying to help people understand their experiences, the answer is obvious.

Science is not always tied up in a neat little bow. Take fibromyalgia, for example. Rheumatologists now accept it as a real disease. Yet, there is no diagnostic test that can identify it. It is diagnosed through elimination of other conditions. So are ALL fibro suffers nuts? Are the rheumatologists who diagnose and treat them irresponsible? I don't think so. Can you imagine any competent doctor saying, "The series of symptoms you describe is being reported by millions of others, but because we can't present any tangible evidence of your pain, it doesn't exist. Furthermore, even though there is consistent anecdotal evidence that taking certain measures can help manage the pain, I'm not going to tell you about them because they are unsubstantiated." I don't think so.

How many times have you heard the term "closed-minded skeptic?" I have been called this (often accompanied with a sigh and rolling eyes) when I attempt to provide alternative explanations for hauntings. In general, the term skeptic has a negative connotation, meaning one who doubts something regarded by most as fact. However, in science, a skeptic is one who questions beliefs and tests the reliability of claims by subjecting them to a systematic investigation using scientific methodology. I used to believe orbs in pictures were evidence of spirits. Once I researched facts regarding airborne particles, I changed my mind, based on objective information from several sources. Looking for validation doesn't make one closed-minded. But consistently ignoring rational facts does.

Going back to EMFs possibly affecting people in various ways, I have personally experienced and observed, with fairly consistent correlation, certain affects. So have other people, including credible investigators. Is it hard science? No. But can hard science be applied towards it if enough people document and report such accounts? I say yes. Such anecdotal evidence is a valid starting point on which to base a hypothesis. And the reality is, that's where we currently are in this field: **We are still gathering data**. So dismissing such experiences offhand is counterproductive to valid research.

It is a common misconception that there is one strict scientific method universally applied by all scientists. This has been popularized by elementary school science textbooks, and although the science fair "hypothesis - experiment - conclusion" model is an important part of basic sciences like physics and chemistry, it is not the only way to perform valid science. Many sciences, like astronomy and paleontology do not fit well into this rigid mold. The real process of science is non-linear and complex.

CREEPY CORNERS

Our human creativity and curiosity inspire exploration: asking questions, making observations, sharing data and ideas. In gathering data, a hypothesis is either supported or opposed. If opposed, does that mean the end of it? No. It can inspire a revised or new hypothesis, or inspire entirely new assumptions which then can be applied to the process. Community analysis and feedback is a vital part. This includes peer review, replication, and discussion which includes coming up with new questions and ideas and theory building. To me, this is exactly what many science-based paranormal researchers are currently doing.

There are ongoing experiments by credentialed scientists regarding the effects of EMFs on human physiology. (The operative word being "ongoing"). In my humble layman opinion, some studies do suggest there is a correlation between certain fields and reported paranormal experiences. And to the Labcoats: yes, I know correlation does not imply a causal link and this is not scientific proof. I would like to point out that technically, scientific proof is found only in mathematics and logic. There is no final proven knowledge in science. Scientific theories, even in physics, are changeable as new discoveries are made. For example, researches at CERN (the European organization for Nuclear Research) recently reported that they recorded particles moving faster than the speed of light. While this is currently being assessed by other agencies, keep it in mind when critics of paranormal research stomp their feet and assert that ghosts or psychokinesis *can't* exist because they break the laws of physics.

Dr. Michael Persinger is a neuroscientist who has conducted experiments regarding magnetic fields and the brain. He hypothesizes that magnetic fields can create interhemopheric intrusions between the two hemispheres of the brain, which can produce hallucinations. In his experiments, in which he applied weak fluctuating magnetic fields to subjects, 80% reported sensing a "presence" in the room with them. The nature of the perceived presences seemed to be subjective. Those with religious or spiritual beliefs were more susceptible to feeling a spiritual experience. Those with no such beliefs still experienced perceptions induced by the field. Richard Dawkins (a well-known atheist and skeptic) reported feeling dizzy and strange sensations in his limbs - which have been reported by people in supposed haunted locations where high EMFs were found. One interesting case involved a man who claimed he experienced a haunting where he saw an apparition. When he visited Persinger's lab and was exposed to the fields, he saw the same exact ghost. The strength of the field Persinger used was no more than what a standard hand-held hair dryer produces. So since it's fairly common to find appliances in households that give off higher fields, it is reasonable to suppose similar experiences may be induced by these fields. One can suppose that perhaps the fields make a person more "psychic", but based on how the subjects' personal beliefs corresponded with their type of experiences, I personally don't believe that is the case.

Dr. William Roll was a psychologist and parapsychologist (he conducted parapsychology research for eight years at Oxford University). While his initial research concerned the correlation of psychokinesis and so-called poltergeist activity (after researching over 100 poltergeist cases he theorized that epileptic activity triggered recurrent spontaneous psychokinesis in the subjects) he later went on to study the correlation between reported "hauntings" and electromagnetic fields. He measured magnetic currents from the earth, and from sources that give off natural electromagnetic currents, such as streams, wells, and mineral deposits and found in places of reported hauntings there were higher than normal readings. He also found that these types of occurrences, where people reported feeling a presence and seeing shadows and apparitions, were associated with anomalous electromagnetic and geomagnetic disturbances. In addition, high EMFs from man-made sources within a house also were found to be a factor in some cases, and might explain why one house may be experiencing a haunting, while the house next door is ghost-free. One of the cases he worked on was profiled on *Unsolved Mysteries* in the 1980's. It involved a little girl in Georgia who could see and talk to ghosts. Dr. Roll believed there was nothing paranormal about the case, and collected data suggesting the geomagnetic and electromagnetic fields induced her experiences. He also believed some of the claims to be connected to psychological factors. But it is interesting, that like Persinger's subjects, the family's belief system colored their perception of the experience. I recently watched an update on the family. Since working with Dr. Roll, the family's pastor got involved and concluded the family was plagued by demons. So they went with that theory. Not to be cynical, but what would get somebody more attention: EM fields or demons? Which would get more viewers for a TV show?

Both Persinger's and Roll's work remains controversial. Even if their findings are valid, it is difficult to apply them practically out in the field. Persinger's experiments were confined to a lab, whereas most paranormal investigators conduct their research in private homes and businesses. Roll's data was collected at sites of reported hauntings, but it is impossible to anticipate and control all possible factors that can affect the environment and the readings, especially for the average paranormal investigator and their clients. However, their work set a foundation for current studies being conducted.

The following information is extracted from an excellent article by Maurice Townsend found on the Association for Scientific Study of Anomalous Phenomena's website (see link in *Sources and Recommended Reading* at the end of this book). Dr. Jason Braithwaite coined the term Experience-

tectonic strain producing extremely localized surface electromagnetic disturbances through piezoelectricity in the sub surface rocks. (For a demonstration in piezoelectricity, get yourself a pack of Wint-O-Green Lifesavors, go in a dark room with a mirror and bite on down on a piece of the candy. That spark you see is produced by the stress and fracture of piezoelectric materials in the candy). Again, these fields seem to be too low to produce EIFs. However, Friedemann Freund (scientist at UC San Jose) has suggested electric charges could be induced to flow by pressure to igneous rocks, turning them into temporary semi-conductors. This theory has more promise than piezoelectricity since the electric charges are not cancelled out and move around to produce magnetic fields. The charges are conducted by igneous rock (including granite, diorite and basalt etc.) along or close to fault lines. (Again, this support's Dr. Roll's observations with quartz and mica deposits and underground streams).

Even with some data supporting natural EMFs as a possible source of Experience Inducing Fields, at this point, studies indicate man-made EMFs are much more likely candidates. The most significant source of EIF magnetic fields is movement or mechanical vibration of magnetic materials, i.e.: metals with a high magnetic permeability such as iron and steel. This distorts the earth's magnetic field around them. Examples sited: Sheets of steel vibrating in the wind, iron bed frames vibrating from passing traffic. I have also read where a passing truck, trains and moving elevators can also create these fields. Nearby factories or power plants can create magnetically dense areas. Common examples found within households are electrical motors used in central heating and AC refrigerators, fans, and washing machines and other appliances. So obviously, homes with a lot of electrical equipment in use may create EIFs. Something to also consider is defective equipment. It is possible, in malfunctioning equipment, that fields can leak to nearby conductors, such as water pipes. Another finding pertinent to paranormal investigations is that the shape of the source and its angle to the field, as well as the permeability and magnetism of vibrating metal, affects the degree of distortion. This explains why hallucinations would only be experienced in small areas. This is relevant to reports where ghosts are seen (or sensed) only in certain rooms or spots.

So let me revisit my personal experiences relevant to EMFs. One of the most frightening experiences was at a relative's house. I often stayed with them and had no issues at their old house, but in their new home they built, I could never sleep well and had unsettling dreams. In addition, my relatives reported odd experiences and thought it was haunted. So one oppressively hot summer night, I was trying to sleep on top of a bed. Suddenly, I felt the sensation and pressure of someone running their finger from my hip to ankle. Initially, I thought it was one of my relatives playing a prank. I quickly flipped on the lamp but found no one there. I admit, it freaked me out and I kept the light on for the rest of the night. However, after learning about EIFs, now I am certain what I experienced wasn't paranormal because there is an active fault line running right along the property. Add a ceiling fan running above and me tossing and turning on a bed with steel springs, and there is a recipe for an EIF. Some years later, I complained to a chiropractor that I was suffering from frequent nightmares. I had tried a lot of suggestions: no alcohol after dinner, stopping certain medications, no TV before bedtime, massage therapy, herbs, etc. with no success. She gave me information on the effects of high EMFs and suggested I remove any sources from my room. Since I had an interest in the paranormal anyway, I ordered a cheap EMF detector and found that my clock radio, which was located on a stand next to my pillow, gave off "unsafe" levels of EMFs. So I moved it to the opposite side of the room. Within a week or so, the nightmares stopped and now I rarely have them. Are these anecdotal experiences proof that EMFs affect us? No. Do they indicate a relevant connection to the studies discussed? Possibly, so we shouldn't ignore them.

The paranormal field is suffering from counterproductive arguments from both ends of the spectrum. On one side, there are those who come from a purely metaphysical perspective who refuse to accept science-based data because it challenges their spiritual beliefs or agendas. On the other side, you have hard-core scientists who ignore compelling data because it doesn't fit into a narrow strict methodology. These mindsets fail to get us any closer to valid answers and both sides can benefit from applying a little more common sense.

TRUTH AND CONSEQUENCES

As mentioned in the first chapter, people want to believe in the paranormal for various reasons. Some of these are deeply personal. It can be a delicate balance for investigators who recognize common causes for some seemingly paranormal events.

It is very hard to compete against cognitive bias. It is natural for people to draw conclusions based on belief, expectations, conditioning, or even preference. We are uncomfortable when our conclusions are challenged, even when concrete facts proving otherwise are presented. This is a common occurrence in the paranormal field. It amazes me that some prefer to believe in something that terrifies them because it reinforces a belief system. One example is hypnagogic hallucinations. You can present people with this well-documented medical condition, but some will still insist a demon is attacking them at night because somehow, the belief serves a purpose for them. Another example I often encounter is when clients or investigators present an anomalous photo for analysis. Team 1 says it's dust. Team 2 says it's dust. Team 3 says its dust. But Team 4 says "good catch" of a ghost. So the photographer goes with Team 4's "validation", because that's what they wanted to hear.

When presented with alternative explanations for their seemingly paranormal experiences, some people believe there is also the implication that they are either stupid, lying or crazy. This is untrue. As explained earlier, there are common environmental and physiological factors that can impair a healthy and sane person's perception.

I am often asked if doing science-based investigating has taken the "magic" out of ghost stories for me. I admit, it has. But I still enjoy them, even if I now listen from a different perspective. And, as I mentioned before, I don't believe science has found all the answers regarding the paranormal, so I am still open to the possibility that ghosts exist.

Sometimes people want us, as paranormal investigators, to validate their belief in ghosts. Even if we explain to them that we're not able to do that at this point, they really want us to tell them their house is haunted. In the cases where they just want to have a good story to tell their friends, I don't feel that bad. But then there are cases when they want us to give them proof that a loved one is still around. This is very difficult, at least for me. As much as I value the truth, I am a compassionate person and can understand how they feel.

By now, it should be crystal clear that I don't believe orbs are ghosts. However, despite all the evidence to the contrary, some books, groups, psychics, books, TV shows, ghost tours, etc. are still promoting them as such. So it is a really touchy situation when people approach me with an orb picture and they believe it's evidence of a departed loved one. If they ask me as a friend, I will simply tell them if that's what they believe and it gives them comfort, then that's all that matters. But if they want my opinion as a paranormal investigator, I have to be honest and tell them orbs have known natural causes. As you would expect, they are disappointed with my answer. But it raises a bigger issue about our beliefs and faith: if we truly believe in an afterlife, why do we need a picture or any other physical proof?

I admit that I want some kind of proof. I want to know that when I die, the memories and experiences that make me Carolyn won't die, too. Like the night I first met my husband. The first time I swam in the ocean. When I made first chair in All-State Orchestra. When my best friend and I got lost and wound up at the Gilroy Garlic Festival, giggling like crazy. When I brought home my kitties from an animal shelter. Yes, I make no apologies that I want some part of my consciousness to survive. Even more so, I want to believe that I will be reunited – at least in some form – with my departed loved ones who I miss so dearly.

But as much as we want such proof, could there be a higher purpose at work behind why we may never find it? Maybe if we aren't certain that a part of us really survives death, we will better appreciate and value the life we've been given. Perhaps if we're not sure we will be reunited with those we love, we will never take them for granted and will remember to tell them, "I love you".

CHAPTER 5: STEPPING INTO THE LIGHT (CONCLUSION)

Have I found the answers I've been looking for? Not yet. But I have learned a lot from visiting a variety of alleged haunted locations, and daring myself to explore their dark, creepy corners. Because I like problem-solving, I have enjoyed discovering natural causes for many common claims. On the other side of that, I love that at least for now, there are still some mysteries yet to be solved. I have had fun trying out investigative techniques and experiments for myself (even if I look kinda nuts talking to a flashlight). But the most rewarding part for me so far, is that I have met great people along the way, with whom to discuss – and debate - ideas that may help us on our mutual quests.

So where do we go from here? For my part, I look forward to participating in more investigations as well as learning more from fellow researchers. I will continue my search to find the truth in paranormal claims.

How about you? I hope you are eager to research the topics discussed in this book for yourself. Please take a look at the resources listed at the end of this book and visit my blog to check out links to informative articles. Are there ghosts? When you find the answer, please let me know.

CAROLYN DOUGHERTY
PICTURE GALLERY

Devil's Den at Gettysburg. Gettysburg is considered by many paranormal enthusiasts to be one of the most haunted locations. The bloody battle fought here changed the course of the Civil War. (Carolyn Dougherty)

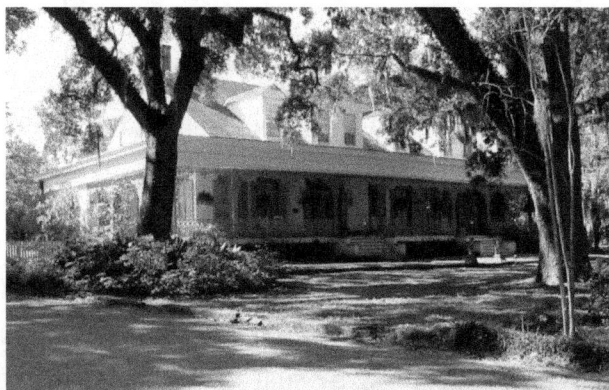

The Myrtles Plantation in Louisiana. Do ghosts of children haunt this place? I don't know, but it's still a beautiful location worth visiting. (Carolyn Dougherty)

CREEPY CORNERS

Cemetery in Plymouth Rock. Cemeteries have a reputation for being haunted. However, they are tricky places to conduct valid investigations. There are too many factors that can contaminate video and audio. Always get permission to investigate. (Carolyn Dougherty)

Burlington County Prison in New Jersey. This is where some convicts met their death at the end of a rope. Are they still imprisoned here? (Carolyn Dougherty)

Buffalo Central Terminal. This is a grand building from a grand era. Are there ghosts here, still waiting for their loved ones to arrive? (Carolyn Dougherty)

Place d'Armes Hotel in New Orleans. Nestled in the French Quarter, this hotel used to be an orphanage. Some say the children remain here, playing ghostly pranks on guests and staff. (Carolyn Dougherty)

CREEPY CORNERS

GLOSSARY

Ambient noise: also known as background noise. It is the pervasive noise in a given environment.

Apophenia: is the experience of perceiving patterns or meaning in meaningless data.

Autokinesis: a visual illusion in which a small point of light in a dark environment appears to move

Bigfoot: see *Sasquatch*.

Clairvoyance: the ability to obtain information about objects, people, events or locations via means beyond the known senses.

Cognitive bias: the tendency to make errors in judgment due to preconceived notions or expectations, even when factual evidence should lead to a different conclusion.

Cold Reading: a series of techniques used to determine and express details about another person, in a manner that suggests the reader "knows" personal information about the subject.

Crytptomnesia: a forgotten memory, that when later recalled seems like a new or original thought.

Cryptozoology: the search for and study of animals whose existence is in dispute or unsubstantiated

Demon: a malevolent spirit. In some religious teachings, can be a fallen angel or an evil human spirit. Derived from the Greek word daemon, originally denoted a spirit or spiritual being, with no negative connotations.

EIFs: Experience Inducing Fields. Electromagnetic fields that can affect the brain, causing sensations and even hallucinations that seem like genuine paranormal experiences.

CAROLYN DOUGHERTY

EMFs: Electromagnetic fields. A force generated by electric charge with both electric and magnetic components.

EMF meter: A meter that detects and measures electromagnetic fields as well as fluctuations within those fields.

ESP: Extrasensory Perception. Communication or perception by means other than the physical senses

EVPs: Electronic Voice Phenomena. A voice of unknown origin that is not audible at the time, but is recorded onto to an electronic device and then heard during playback.

False Positives: In paranormal research, video or audio artifacts that are misinterpreted as something paranormal. Also applies to seemingly anomalous EMF spikes that, in reality, have known causes.

Galea Aperneurotica: muscles of the scalp that cover the cranium. Has nothing to do with the paranormal, I just like saying it.

Ghost: In most cultures, a spirit, soul or consciousness of a deceased person

Hypnagogia: the transitional state between sleep and wakefulness

Hypnagogic Hallucinations: vivid visual, audio, tactile or olfactory hallucinations experienced while in the hypnagogic state

Ideomoter Effect: when a subject makes a movement unconsciously. Such movements can be influenced by suggestion and expectation.

Inattentional blindness: also called perceptional blindness, an inability to perceive something that is within one's direct perceptual field because one is focused on something else or attending to a task.

CREEPY CORNERS

Incubus: Male form of a succubus.   Good to know the difference, especially if one is a paranormal TV personality trying to summon one on national television.

Infrared: electromagnetic radiation wavelengths just greater than the red end of the visible light spectrum. Emitted partially by heated objects.

Infrasound: a frequency below the audile range of human hearing, under 20 Hz.

IR illuminator: Infrared illuminator. Emits light in the infrared frequency range, enhancing images in very low light, used for night vision settings in cameras.

ITC: Instrumental Transcommunication. Communication with spirits through electronic devices

Lens flare: light reflecting through the camera which appears on the image as a haze, starbursts, rings, circles (orbs), typically caused by pointing the camera toward a bright light source.

Long Exposure: in photography, an effect caused when the shutter speed is set at a longer duration, and moving elements will appear blurred or as streaks.   In low light conditions, a point-and-shoot camera will have a slower shutter speed, causing this effect.

Matrixing: *see Pareidolia*

Medium: not small or large. Just kidding, see *psychic.*

Misperception: occurs when the brain misinterprets sensory information

Night Hag: see *sleep paralysis, succubus*

Optical Illusion: shapes, shadows, colors, line distortions that can lead the brain to misinterpret visual information or cues

Orbs: camera or video artifacts that appear as balls of light, but in reality are a product of reflection off of airborne particles such as dust, moisture, and bugs.

Orb zone: the area in front of a camera where the flash (or illuminator, in case of video) illuminates airborne particles that are closer than the point of focus.

Ovilus: also known as a Puck, is an electronic speech-synthesis devise which generates words based on electromagnetic waves.

Paranormal: general term for experiences that are outside the range of normal experience or scientific explanation.

Parapsychologist: a person with degrees in sciences such as psychology, anthropology, or physics who applies science to formal parapsychological studies. Recently, it is more broadly used to describe anyone who studies the paranormal.

Parapsychology: study of claims and experiences of paranormal phenomena; the general scope of research involving ESP (extrasensory perception) telepathy, precognition, clairvoyance, psychokinesis, near-death experiences and apparitional experiences

Pareidolia: misperception in which vague or random images or sounds are misinterpreted as a meaningful pattern. Common examples are seeing shapes in clouds or hearing words in ambient noise.

Poltergeist: German term meaning "noisy ghost". Spirit activity involving knocks, scratching, pushing, vocalization, throwing objects, starting fires, etc.. Now generally considered by parapsychologists to be a product of psychic phenomena.

Possession: the state of being under the power or control of a supernatural entity

Precognition: knowledge of an event via extrasensory perception before it occurs.

CREEPY CORNERS

Psi: term relating to psychic phenomena or ability

Psychic: 1. Adjective; relating to phenomena or abilities that are unexplained, usually in reference to telepathy or clairvoyance. 2. Noun; a person considered or claiming to have psychic powers, also called a medium.

Psychokinesis: (**PK**) the ability to move or influence an object through psychic means, believed by parapsychologists to be the cause of poltergeist activity.

Psychosomatic: relating to physical symptoms caused by mental or emotional disturbances

Sasquatch: A legendary creature found in tribal lore across North America, believed to be an undiscovered primate.

Sleep Paralysis: a sleep disorder in which the subject experiences an inability to move either during sleep onset or upon awakening. Sometimes accompanied by hypnagogic hallucinations, including sensing, seeing or hearing a presence, the feeling someone or something is sitting on them, feeling suffocated, or even assaulted. Also called the Night Hag syndrome, since before advances in modern medicine, people attributed the phenomena to such supernatural creatures.

Spirit Box: (also called Franks box, ghost box): a device or altered radio (Shack Hack) that sweeps radio frequencies in which ghosts supposedly can somehow anticipate and pick out words to communicate.

Succubus: originating in medieval folklore, a female demon who drains men's souls by having sexual intercourse with them.

Telepathy: communication of thoughts or ideas through extrasensory means.

Vortex: supposed doorways or portals to other dimensions that are made up of energy and/or light. Often mistaken in pictures of hair, spider webs, thread or lint that fall into the orb zone.

White noise: a heterogeneous mixture of sound waves extending over a wide frequency range. Also, a constant background noise that may drown out other sounds.

Zombie: 1. Me, before my first cup of coffee. 2. A reanimated corpse, under the control of a living agent or by possession of a malevolent entity. More recently in popular culture, the reanimated corpses are a result of an apocalyptical virus.

CREEPY CORNERS
SOURCES AND RECOMMENDED READING

Books:

An Illustrated Encyclopaedia of Traditional Symbols by J.C. Cooper

A Paranormal Casebook : Ghost Hunting in the New Millennium by Loyd Auerback

The Believing Brain: From and Gods and Politics and Conspiracies --- How we Construct them as Beliefs and Reinforce Them as Truths by Michael Shermer

Dictionary of Mysticism and the Esoteric Traditions by Nevill Drury

Ghost Research 101: Investigating Haunted Homes by Dave Juliano

Ghosts: Appearances of the Dead and Cultural Transformation by R. C. Finucane

Ghost Science by Vince Wilson

Ghost Tech by Vince Wilson

Orbs or Dust? A Practical Guide to False-Positive Evidence by Kenneth Biddle

Paranormal Pub by Patrick Doyle

Paranormal Technology: Understanding the Science of Ghost Hunting by David M. Roundtree

Parapsychology: The Controversial Science by Richard S. Broughton, Ph.D

Spook: Science Tackles the Afterlife by Mary Roach

Strange Frequencies: A Practical Guide to Paranormal Technology by Craig Telesha

CAROLYN DOUGHERTY

The Weiser Field Guide to Ghosts, Apparitions, Spirits, Spectral Lights, and Other Hauntings of History and Legend by Raymond Buckland

Links:

Association for the Scientific Study of Anomalous Phenomena: www.assap.ac.uk/newsite/htmlfiles/Articles.html

Carolyn's Creepy Corner: http://carolynscreepycorner.blogspot.com

The Ghost Hunter Store: http://theghosthunterstore.com/

The Ghost Society, LLC: http://thegsny.com

The Haunted Cottage: http://www.thehauntedcottage.com/

I Hunt Ghosts: http://ihuntghosts.com/

It's Haunted: http://www.itshaunted.com/

Jim's Destinations: http://www.jimsdestinations.com/

Massachusetts Paranormal Research Society: http://massprs.com/

Midnite Walkers Paranormal Research Society: http://midnite-walkers.com/

Midwest Preternatural Research: http://www.midwestpreternaturalresearch.com/

MyPara Paranormal Social Network: http://www.mypara.net/

Paranormal Investigator and Research Association: http://home.comcast.net/~parainvestigator/Index/Main.html

River Cities Paranormal Society: Wisconsin affiliate: http://www.rcpswi.com/ and Kansas City affiliate: http://www.rcpskc.com/index.html

Viper Paranormal: http://www.viperparanormal.com/

150

CREEPY CORNERS

Media:

The Ghost Society, LLC Podcast:
http://www.thegsny.com/Our_Show.html

How To Be A Ghost Hunter:
http://www.youtube.com/user/screamfreak79

Maine Ghost Hunters Radio Show:
http://www.maineghosthunters.org/media/

Paranormal Generation: http://paranormalgeneration.com/

Reputable Hauntings: http://www.blogtalkradio.com/massprs

CAROLYN DOUGHERTY

ABOUT THE AUTHOR

Carolyn Dougherty is a former educator who has had a life-long interest in the paranormal. She was a lead investigator and Director of Research for The Ghost Society LLC and primary writer for the first season of their podcast. She was the assistant editor and contributing writer for *MyPara Paranormal Magazine*.

While she's been called eccentric, Carolyn is mostly harmless. She lives in Upstate New York with her patient and understanding husband, Dan, and their extremely spoiled cat.

Please visit her blog at:
CAROLYNSCREEPYCORNER.BLOGSPOT.COM

CREEPY CORNERS

PRAISE FOR CAROLYN'S CREEPY CORNER

carolynscreepycorner.blogspot.com

"As a serious paranormal investigator and researcher I look at the evidence presented by other paranormal teams very hard. I do this because I want to help educate new teams and minimize the negative effect some of the not so serious teams have on the field of paranormal research. Fortunately I am not alone in this quest. With exceptional content added in every blog, and some of the most educational paranormal links on the internet; Carolyn Dougherty's Creepy Corner educates and entertains. If you are serious about paranormal investigation or just want to learn more about ghosts; I strongly recommend Carolyn's Creepy Corner".

--**Mike St. Clair**

VIPER- Founder

How to be a Ghost Hunter- **Producer**

"There is a ton of misinformation out there in regards to paranormal investigating. The problem is that many groups just copy what they see or hear on TV, or what they see everyone else doing, without doing any of their own research. If everyone else is doing it then it must be true, right? Wrong.

If people repeat things often enough, they become accepted as common knowledge. It's the same with ghost hunting. A lot of groups just copy what they see or hear repeated everywhere, even though it's false. That's why it's important to do your own research.

Carolyn's Creepy Corner is a great place to start. It's one of my favorite blogs, and a great resource for anyone who wants to be a better ghost hunter. The author, who has been exploring the field for over 20 years and believes the majority of paranormal claims likely have natural explanations, does a really good job researching and is trying to educate people about some of the misinformation and mistaken evidence that's out there.

The author writes about topics ranging from common misperceptions, false positives, "certified ghost hunters", paranormal profiteers, theories, and methods. I liked where she investigated a popular haunted location that has appeared on several TV shows. But when she talked to a local historian herself, it turned out that much of the history that was presented on the shows had been changed or outright fabricated to make the story more sensational for TV. This is something I've encountered myself with another TV show, and I think it's a good lesson for anyone who takes what they see on TV at face value.

I think that Carolyn's Creepy Corner is doing a lot of good for the paranormal field, and I would highly recommend it to anyone who thinks that all you need to be a ghost hunter is just to imitate what you see on TV".

- **Matt Schenk**

Co-Founder of Midwest Preternatural Society

Cast Member of *Paranormal Generation*

CREEPY CORNERS

"Carolyn is fine tuned to tell it like it is. She takes an edgy, yet direct approach to the field of paranormal investigations and research. This blog is a direct pipeline to the very fundamentals which every paranormal researcher should embrace. Carolyn's blog should be on the list to read of all serious investigators."

- Jonathan Wood,

Founder, River Cities Paranormal Society

Owner, MyPara.net

"In a nutshell, this blog is Honest, Blunt and filled with Common Sense; qualities rarely seen in the paranormal community. Carolyn offers a no-nonsense opinion on popular topics that focuses on the facts rather than guesswork or biases. She points out and discusses common mistakes, and offers researched information and suggestions...all with a delightful attitude and a laugh here and there. Very well done."

- Kenneth Biddle
Author, *Orbs or Dust: A Practical Guide to False Positives*

Image by Tkay Anderson

CAROLYN DOUGHERTY

COSMIC PANTHEON PRESS

Cosmic Pantheon Press - the publishing company for the next generation of authors

Books from Cosmic Pantheon Press and its writers are focused on the spiritual and scientific future of humankind while simultaneously visiting our past for the purpose of intellectual enlightenment.

Titles from Cosmic Pantheon Press focus on everything from American and World History to some of the mysteries of nature including the paranormal and supernatural.

HISTORY

- Read about great people and places.
- Explore moments from the past that changed the outcome of human events.

THE UNEXPLAINED

- Learn the science and techniques of modern day ghost investigators.
- Gain insight into the nature of UFOs and why they may have visited Earth already.
- Ponder your own psychic potential!

PUBLISH WITH US

We are always looking for new and creative writers with exciting ideas. Are you one of our future writers? Visit the CONTACT US section of our site and find out! We are looking forward to hearing from you!

www.cosmicpantheon.com

www.ingramcontent.com/pod-product-compliance
Lightning Source LLC
LaVergne TN
LVHW051125080426
835510LV00018B/2231